Planning and Enabling Learning
in the
Lifelong Learning Sector

Ann Gravells

Susan Simpson

LearningMatters

First published in 2008 by Learning Matters Ltd.

British Library Cataloguing in Publication Data
A CIP record for this book is available from the British Library.

ISBN: 978 1 84445 170 8

Cover design by Topics – The Creative Partnership
Project management by Deer Park Productions, Tavistock, Devon
Typeset by Pantek Arts Ltd, Maidstone, Kent
Printed and bound in Great Britain by Bell & Bain Ltd, Glasgow

Learning Matters Ltd
33 Southernhay East
Exeter EX1 1NX
Tel: 01392 215560
info@learningmatters.co.uk
www.learningmatters.co.uk

CONTENTS

ACKNOWLEDGEMENTS

The authors would like to thank the following for their support and encouragement while they were writing this book:

Jenny Davis
Kate Esmond
Peter Frankish
Bob Gravells
Billy Harrison
Julia Morris
Clare Weaver

The learners and staff of the teacher/training department at Bishop Burton College and North East Lincolnshire Council Adult Community Learning Service in Grimsby.

The authors and publisher would like to thank the following for permission to reproduce copyright material:

Belbin Associates
Lifelong Learning UK

Ann Gravells is a lecturer in teacher training at Bishop Burton College in East Yorkshire. She has 24 years' experience of teaching in further education.

Ann is a consultant to City & Guilds for various projects and is an External Verifier for the teacher training qualifications. She has developed International Qualifications in Teaching and Training in Hong Kong, India and Sri Lanka.

Ann holds a Masters in Educational Management, a PGCE, a Degree in Education, and a City & Guilds Medal of Excellence for teaching. She is the author of *Preparing to Teach in the Lifelong Learning Sector* and *Delivering Adult Learning*.

Susan Simpson is a teacher in teacher training at the North East Lincolnshire Council's Adult Community Learning Service in Grimsby. She has 25 years' experience of teaching in compulsory and post-16 education.

Susan is a curriculum manager for Education and Training, ICT and Business Administration and Law. She developed, managed and taught adult education programmes in Botswana for 10 years. Susan has also presented at regional level for teacher training and nationally for ICT Skills for Life.

Susan holds a post graduate Diploma in Management Studies, BA (Hons) in Further Education and Training, and Certificate in Education (Hons) in Business Studies and Economics.

The authors welcome any comments from readers; please e-mail consult@ anngravells.co.uk

In this chapter you will learn about:

● the structure of the book and how to use it;

● Lifelong Learning professional teaching standards;

● Associate Teacher and Qualified Teacher status;

● teaching qualifications in the Lifelong Learning Sector;

● the minimum core;

● the Institute for Learning.

The structure of the book and how to use it

This book has been specifically written for teachers who are working towards Associate or Qualified Teacher status in the Learning and Skills sector (ATLS and QTLS).

The book is structured in chapters which relate to the content of the Planning and Enabling Learning unit of both the Certificate and Diploma in Teaching in the Lifelong Learning Sector. It builds upon the content of the book *Preparing to Teach in the Lifelong Learning Sector* by Ann Gravells. You can work logically through the book or just look up relevant aspects within the chapters that relate to areas of your teaching and learning.

There are activities to enable you to think about how you teach, and examples to help you understand the process of teaching and learning.

At the end of each chapter is a list of references and sources of further information, enabling you to research relevant topics by using textbooks, publications and/or the internet.

Each chapter is cross-referenced to the new overarching professional standards for teachers, tutors and trainers in the Lifelong Learning Sector. Throughout this book, the generic term *teacher* is used. References to the *minimum core* are listed at the end of each chapter; Appendix 2 contains the full list.

Chapter 7 contains sample documents and pro formas that you might wish to use when teaching. If you are an in-service teacher, do check with your organisation first in case they have particular documents they require you to use. If you are pre-service, these documents will give you a good idea of what you could use when teaching.

The appendices contain the Planning and Enabling Learning standards, minimum core elements, tips for teaching, a list of teaching and learning resources and a useful list of educational abbreviations and acronyms.

The index will help you quickly locate useful topics.

Lifelong Learning professional teaching standards

In September 2007, standards came into effect for all new teachers in the Lifelong Learning Sector who teach on Government-funded programmes in England. This includes all post-16 education, including further education, adult and community learning, work-based learning and offender education.

Teachers in the Lifelong Learning Sector should value all learners individually and equally. They are committed to lifelong learning and professional development and strive for continuous improvement through reflective practice. The key purpose of the teacher is to create effective and stimulating opportunities for learning through high-quality teaching that enables the development and progression of all learners.

The full standards encompass six domains:

A   Professional Values and Practice;
B   Learning and Teaching;
C   Specialist Learning and Teaching;
D   Planning for Learning;
E   Assessment for Learning;
F   Access and Progression.

The standards can be accessed at: http://www.lluk.org.uk/documents/professional_standards_for_itts_020107.pdf

The chapters in this book are cross-referenced to these standards. As you progress through the teaching qualifications, you will need to meet all the relevant criteria relating to the *scope*, *knowledge* and *practice* required in your job role (referenced by: S for *scope*, K for *knowledge* or P for *practice* within the chapters).

The new qualifications for teachers in the Lifelong Learning Sector have been developed based upon the Qualifications and Credit Framework (QCF) model which has mandatory and optional units of assessment at different levels, and different credit values. The units and credits can be built up to form relevant qualifications over time.

The teaching qualifications start at Level 3 on the QCF and can be obtained through an awarding body (AB) or higher education institution (HEI).

The European Commission has defined lifelong learning as:

All purposeful learning activity, undertaken on an ongoing basis with the aim of improving knowledge, skills and competence.

http://www.education.gov.mt/edu/edu_division/life_long_learning/introduction.htm

You may already have taken the Preparing to Teach in the Lifelong Learning Sector (PTLLS) Award and now be progressing to the Certificate in Teaching in the Lifelong Learning Sector (CTLLS) or the Diploma in Teaching in the Lifelong Learning Sector (DTLLS). These qualifications are therefore a purposeful activity which you are undertaking on an ongoing basis with the aim of improving your knowledge, skills and competence as a teacher.

It is important to continually develop and improve your skills throughout your teaching career, not only in the context of teaching, but also in your subject specialist area. You may be required to hold relevant subject qualifications at a certain level, as well as a teaching qualification appropriate to your job role.

Associate Teacher and Qualified Teacher status

Lifelong Learning UK (LLUK) has identified two distinct and important teacher roles in the Further Education sector in England, for which there are Government regulations:

- an *associate teaching* role, which has fewer teaching responsibilities and which will be performed by those who are expected to gain the status of Associate Teacher, Learning and Skills (ATLS);

- a *full teaching* role, which represents the full range of responsibilities performed by those who are expected to gain the status of Qualified Teacher, Learning and Skills (QTLS).

These roles were identified through extensive research into teacher roles in the sector. From September 2007, it is no longer the amount of *time* that someone teaches that determines which teaching qualification(s) should be undertaken, but their *role* as a teacher. All those who teach, even on a part-time basis, will be required to undertake a teaching qualification appropriate for either an *associate* teacher role or a *full* teacher role.

The two teaching roles have been described in the Further Education Teachers' Qualifications (England) Regulations (2007) in the following ways:

Associate teaching role means a teaching role that carries significantly less than the full range of teaching responsibilities ordinarily carried out in a full teaching role (whether on a full-time, part-time, fractional, fixed term, temporary or agency basis) and does not require the teacher to demonstrate an extensive range of knowledge, understanding and application of curriculum development, curriculum innovation or curriculum delivery strategies.

> *Full teaching role means a teaching role that carries the full range of teaching responsibilities (whether on a full-time, part-time, fractional, fixed term, temporary or agency basis) and requires the teacher to demonstrate an extensive range of knowledge, understanding and application of curriculum development, curriculum innovation or curriculum delivery strategies.*
>
> http://www.legislation.gov.uk/si/si2007/20072264.htm

To gain *associate* or *full* teacher status, you need to register with the Institute for Learning (IfL). This is the professional body for teachers, trainers, tutors and trainee teachers in the Learning and Skills sector. You must achieve the relevant teaching qualification for your job role within the required time period, and fulfil the continuing professional development (CPD) requirements, which may include passing tests in literacy, numeracy and information communication technology (ICT). This registration can be completed online at www.ifl.ac.uk.

Teaching qualifications in the Lifelong Learning Sector

There are three main teaching qualifications:

- Preparing to Teach in the Lifelong Learning Sector (PTLLS);

- Certificate in Teaching in the Lifelong Learning Sector (CTLLS);

- Diploma in Teaching in the Lifelong Learning Sector (DTLLS).

All new teachers, whether in an associate role or full teacher role, must undertake the Preparing to Teach in the Lifelong Learning Sector (PTLLS) Award at the beginning of their career. This can be as a discrete award or embedded in the Certificate or Diploma in Teaching in the Lifelong Learning Sector qualifications. Higher Education Institutions can still use the terms Certificate in Education and Postgraduate Certificate in Education. The content is the same as for the Diploma, but it may be offered at a higher level.

This book covers the content of the Planning and Enabling Learning unit of the Certificate and Diploma, and extends the content of the book by Ann Gravells *Preparing to Teach in the Lifelong Learning Sector* (2008).

The minimum core

All teachers should have a knowledge and understanding of literacy, language, numeracy, and information and communication technology (ICT) skills. These are known as the *minimum core* and are integrated into the Planning and Enabling Learning unit of the Certificate and Diploma qualifications. The personal skills aspects of the minimum core will enable you to effectively fulfil your role as a professional teacher. However, the minimum core is not only concerned with your own skills in these subjects; it is also about being able to develop these skills in your learners.

The chapters of this book integrate aspects of the minimum core; however, you should take responsibility for researching these further and ensuring you meet the standards. You might like to take additional learning programmes if, for example, your computer skills need further development or you feel your spelling and grammar need to be improved. When you are teaching, your learners will trust and believe you. If you spell words incorrectly in a handout or on the board, your learners will think the spelling is correct because you are their teacher. If you are aiming for QTLS status, you may need to pass external tests in these subjects before you can obtain your status.

The Institute for Learning

The Institute for Learning (IfL) is the professional body for teachers, trainers, tutors and trainee in the Learning and Skills sector. It is operated by members for members, and celebrates the diverse nature of the sector, including: Adult and Community Learning, Emergency and Public Services, Further Education Colleges, Ministry of Defence/Armed Services, the Voluntary Sector and Work-based Learning.

Under the 2007 Regulations, the IfL provides the mechanism by which teachers register and progress to being Licensed Practitioners. After the relevant teaching qualification has been obtained, teachers will undertake an induction year, known as *professional formation* before acquiring their licence to practise. It will be compulsory for all teachers to register with the IfL and follow a Code of Professional Practice along with the associated disciplinary processes. The Code defines the professional behaviour which, in the public interest, the IfL expects of its members throughout their membership and professional career. The Code can be accessed via the Institute for Learning's website: www.ifl.ac.uk.

While you are working towards your teaching qualifications, it would be extremely useful to have a *mentor*, someone who can help and support you, not only with teaching skills, but also with your specialist subject. Your mentor could observe you teaching and give you developmental feedback.

Summary

In this chapter you have learnt about:

- the structure of the book and how to use it;
- lifelong learning professional teaching standards;
- Associate Teacher and Qualified Teacher status;
- teaching qualifications in the Lifelong Learning Sector;
- the minimum core;
- the Institute for Learning.

References and further information

Gravells A (2008) *Preparing to Teach in the Lifelong Learning Sector* (3rd edn), Exeter: Learning Matters.

LLUK (2006) *New overarching professional standards for teachers, tutors and trainers in the Lifelong Learning Sector*, London: LLUK

Websites

Further Education Teachers' Qualifications (England) Regulations (2007) – http://www.legislation.gov.uk/si/si2007/20072264.htm

Institute for Learning – www.ifl.ac.uk
Lifelong Learning UK – www.lluk.org.uk
Quality Assurance Agency – www.qaa.ac.uk
Qualification Credit Framework – www.qca.org.uk/qca_8150.aspx
Qualifications and Curriculum Authority – www.qca.org.uk

Introduction

In this chapter you will learn about:

- inducting learners;

- icebreaker activities;

- agreeing ground rules with learners;

- the role of initial assessment in the teaching and learning process;

- different methods of initial assessment;

- planning and negotiating learning goals;

- recording learning goals.

There are activities and examples to help you reflect on the above, which will assist your understanding of how to negotiate learning goals.

Guidance to address the minimum core of literacy, language, numeracy and information and communication technology (ICT) is integrated throughout and referenced at the end of the chapter.

Chapter 7 contains useful pro formas you may wish to use.

This chapter contributes towards the following: *scope* (S), *knowledge* (K) and *practice* (P) aspects of the professional standards (A–F domains) for teachers, tutors and trainers in the Lifelong Learning Sector:

AS1, AS3, AK1.1, AP1.1, AK3.1, AP3.1, AK4.2, AP4.2;
BS2, BS3, BS4, BK1.1, BP1.1, BK1.2, BP1.2, BK2.1, BP2.1, BK2.5, BP2.5, BK3.2, BP3.2, BK3.3, BP3.3, BK3.4, BP3.4, BK3.5, BP3.5, BK4.1, BP4.1, BK5.1, BP5.1, BK5.2, BP5.2;
CS1, CS2, CK1.1, CP1.1, CK2.1, CP2.2, CK3.2, CP3.2, CK3.3, CP3.3, CK3.4, CP3.4;
DS1, DS2, DK1.1, DP1.1, DK2.1, DP2.1, DK2.2, DP2.2;
ES1, EK1.1, EP1.1;
FS1, FK1.1, FP1.1, FK1.2, FP1.2, FK4.2, FP4.2.

The standards can be accessed at: http://www.lluk.org.uk/documents/professional _standards_for_itts_020107.pdf

Inducting learners

When you start teaching a programme, you will spend a fair amount of time at the beginning introducing your learners to the programme they have applied for, and to your organisation. This is called an *induction*. The induction process encompasses a range of information and activities preparing your learners for the programme. For example, information, advice, guidance, and initial assessment.

Induction and the initial assessment of your learners could be a key area of your responsibility. By the end of this process both you and your learner should be confident that they are on a programme appropriate for them with a positive outlook towards achieving their learning goals. Your organisation may decide the length of the induction period and what should be covered. You will need to familiarise yourself with the documents; for example, an induction checklist, and the procedures which you will be required to use. As a teacher, you need to know what is expected of you and what is available to you to support your learners. The whole process must reflect the needs of your learners.

Induction aims to develop the learner's independent learning habits, provide knowledge, and signpost towards any relevant support and guidance that's available; for example, a learner may require additional support for a disability they have disclosed to you.

Activity

Think back to the first induction session you experienced as a learner. What activities took place and what information did you receive? How did it help you? Was there anything else that could have been included?

You may have responded by saying that the induction provided important information about the centre, the staff and the programme. You were made aware of the organisation's policies for reporting absence, evacuating the building in an emergency and where the main facilities were. It would have helped if there had been more information about the programme, the assessment of the qualification and the personal time commitment required.

It may be that your learners will have started their relationship with your organisation before you have met them. They may have seen the programme advertised either in a brochure, newspaper or on a website, and made enquiries or attended an open day. They may have formed some opinion already about what they have experienced. This first point of contact is crucial in building the foundations of a good learning experience. Some of your learners will have completed the enrolment procedures, had an interview and received information (either a leaflet or details accessed from the organisation's website) giving a brief outline of the programme and any entry requirements. Your organisation may produce a *learner handbook* which will contain all the information the learner needs to know about the organisation. If not, you need to ensure your learners have all the relevant information they need.

However, during the first session with you there may be some learners who have not yet completed all the enrolment paperwork, paid their fees etc, and you may have to plan in sufficient time for this to be completed.

When planning your induction programme it is important you acknowledge that literacy, language, numeracy and information communication technology (ICT) are important for the achievement of qualifications. Many learners will have struggled with English and maths at school and may therefore experience a lack of confidence in these areas. You will need to ensure your own skills in these areas are adequate to support your learners.

The first stage of the induction process will inform your learners in two main areas:

- *housekeeping and related procedures*:
    - toilets, parking, refreshments, contact information;
    - health and safety, evacuation;
    - policies and procedures which may affect all aspects of their learning experience; for example, equal opportunities policy, complaints policy;
    - notifying an absence or withdrawal from their programme.

- *the programme*:
    - entry requirements – any specific qualifications or skills and knowledge learners need to have;
    - introduction to the staff team and how to contact them;
    - programme and qualification overview – the aims, in language that learners will understand;
    - time commitment: classes/tutorials/reviews/homework;
    - appropriate resources and specialist support available;
    - assessments to be undertaken, commencing with initial assessment; formative assessment throughout the programme and summative assessment at the end of the programme;
    - expectations: attendance, meeting target dates;
    - signpost/offer guidance to other learning opportunities/support;
    - dates/times/holidays.

By covering the above at the beginning of your induction, learners will recognise very quickly what is required of them. If they are not on the right programme at the right level, they can be guided and supported towards a more appropriate one. It is very important that you contact any learners who do not return after the first session to find out why, and offer support as necessary to guide them elsewhere. Alternatively, they may have been absent for a legitimate reason and just need to be updated on what was missed.

When you commence a session, adopt the habit of *first in, last out* for yourself. You need to allow at least 10 to 15 minutes before the session begins, and after it ends, to give your learners an opportunity to talk to you, and to prepare/tidy your teaching environment. During the induction stage, learners will have a variety of questions they may want to ask you. Some may need reassurance that they will be able to cope, or some may have a particular learning need that they want to tell you about in confidence. You can discover a great deal about your learners during these few minutes and you may be able to allay any fears or find a solution to a problem. This will build your learners' confidence that you are accessible to them, which may affect their decision to return the following session.

Example

Peter has started work as a study support assistant for an Adult Community Learning Service and wants to achieve a qualification. Under the guidance of the teacher, he provides one-to-one support for learners with either disabilities or learning difficulties. He enrolled on the Preparing to Teach in the Lifelong Learning Sector programme and attended the first week. He did not return the second week and e-mailed the teacher to say that after the induction he felt that it was not the right time for him to embark on this programme. An alternative programme was discussed with Peter and it was agreed that the National Vocational Qualification (NVQ) Level 2 in Supporting Teaching and Learning was a more appropriate programme for his present job role. Peter was withdrawn from the PTLLS programme and transferred to the NVQ.

During induction it is very important to inform your learners how the teaching, learning, and assessment activities will take place. The programme may require your learners to access the internet, communicate by e-mail, purchase equipment, or research topics in their own time. Therefore, they will need to be aware of this when commencing.

Icebreaker activities

Traditionally, teachers have used icebreakers at the commencement of a learning programme, to help learners get to know one another. It's a light-hearted, friendly way to introduce learners to each other at the start of a session. However, different types of icebreaker can be used throughout a programme to introduce new topics or energise learners.

Well-chosen icebreakers can ease learners through the discomfort of getting to know others, and the teacher, better. They can help to set a positive atmosphere for learner interaction and encourage interest in the overall learning experience. However, in some circumstances icebreakers need to be used with caution; some of your learners may be very nervous about returning to learning, or experiencing new learning in a new environment with new people. Learners may be worried and anxious at the suggestion of participating in an icebreaker, particularly if they have never come across this concept before, or it has been thrust upon them.

Consider the following when choosing icebreaker activities:

- the size of the group: make sure that the icebreaker you have chosen is manageable for the number of learners;

- the purpose of the icebreaker: will you use it as an opening activity to enable learners to get to know each other better; will you use it as an activity to raise flagging energy levels or encourage creativity? Make it clear to the group what you are asking them to do and why;

- the preparation required: choose simple icebreakers rather than complicated ones. An icebreaker to introduce your learners to each other need not take longer than 10 minutes. Try to practise the activity first before using it with your learners, or at least run through each step so that you are confident it will work effectively;

- the materials required: make a checklist of materials and bring them with you. Be ready to improvise if you forget a crucial item or do not have enough resources;

- the time available: be realistic about time spent on the icebreaker and keep to it. Choose a short, punchy icebreaker to get started, and longer icebreakers when more disclosure is required.

Activity

You have a group of learners, eight of whom have progressed from an introductory programme and know each other very well, and six new learners who do not know anyone. Design an icebreaker activity you would use with them and consider why you have chosen it for this particular group.

You may have decided to place the group into smaller groups of three in each, mixing the existing and new learners. You might have asked them to chat about their expectations of the programme, their hobbies, interests etc. The existing learners can then introduce the others, alleviating any fears of their having to talk in front of a new group for the first time.

Agreeing ground rules with learners

Under the new Professional Standards for Teachers, Tutors and Trainers in the Lifelong Learning Sector your aim will be to create a safe learning environment that promotes tolerance, respect and co-operation between your learners. One of the best ways of achieving this is to develop an agreement with your learners regarding *ground rules*. These are rules that should be agreed by, and followed by, all learners within your group. Involving your learners in the process encourages them to take responsibility and ownership for their own learning. Your learners will learn best in an environment in which they are able to participate, voice their opinions, ask questions and be actively involved in determining how they will learn.

Ground rules should be agreed by the whole group rather than imposed by you. By showing an interest in their decisions, you are communicating with your learners that they are valued as individuals, who bring useful skills and knowledge to the session.

Activity

You have a group of 10 learners who are feeling relaxed and comfortable after their icebreaker. You now ask them to agree some ground rules. What do you think they might suggest?

You might think that they will agree to switch off their mobile phones and arrive on time. However, it might be useful to get them to think about dividing their ground rules into rights and responsibilities; for example:

● *We have a right to*:
  - be treated with respect;
  - be listened to;
  - be assured of confidentiality.

● *We have a responsibility to*:
  - be on time for sessions;
  - not disrupt the session;
  - switch off mobile phones.

It is important to encourage all your learners to express their opinions in the group, providing these are valid and relevant to the programme. However, some learners may take longer to express themselves than others. The group will need to know that decisions made regarding ground rules at the start of the programme may need to be renegotiated or evaluated at a later stage in the programme. This renegotiation process may give those learners who preferred to stay silent at the start an opportunity to participate. You could write the ground rules on flipchart paper and display it each session as a reminder.

Your organisation may have its own learning contract/agreement with written commitments that you, your learner and your organisation will agree to. The negotiated ground rules can be seen as an extension of this to include items which may affect the group as a whole.

You may see this process as a starting point for consultation and negotiation with your learners in other aspects. Involving your learners in making decisions about their programme increases their interest, commitment, motivation and learning.

Activity

You have a group of 12 learners taking an Introduction to Digital Photography programme. Some of the teaching and learning takes place in the ICT suite and there are three visits to external locations to take photographs. The learners have signed your organisation's learning contract and the appropriate health and safety documentation in relation to the visits. You would like the learners to decide on their own code of conduct when they are away from the organisation. What do you think they would include?

You might think they would include arriving punctually at an agreed meeting place, remaining with the group until the end of the visit; bringing and being responsible for their own digital camera and any other equipment; and not taking photographs of members of the public without their permission. Having ground rules like these will ensure the visit goes well.

The role of initial assessment in the teaching and learning process

If you need to visit a doctor's surgery, or take your car for a service you can confidently expect an assessment, diagnosis and remedy. The same approach should be applied when it comes to assessing the needs of your learners and matching them to an appropriate programme and suitable level.

Initial assessment may be the start of your relationship with your learners and you will begin to know what motivates them to learn. For some learners, this will be an opportunity to divulge any concerns or personal (sometimes confidential) information about themselves.

Assessment is an integral part of the learning process. Initial assessment takes place at the commencement of your learners' journey, but is effective only when seen as part of a wider and ongoing process. A key part of initial assessment is to involve your learners in assessing their own skills and knowledge.

> *Assessment should not be something that is done to somebody. The learner must be involved and feel part of the process.*
> Lesley Thom, Training Standards Council (2001)

The role of initial assessment is to identify different kinds of information from your learners when they commence a programme with you. This information will:

- determine your learner's starting point; for example, any skills and knowledge that your learner already has, (this should relate to the subject being taken) and also any literacy, language, numeracy and ICT skills that may be applicable;

- identify whether any information collected needs to be shared with colleagues; for example, your learner may disclose a disability and require additional support;

- secure the best match between your learner and their learning process; for example, the right level. Some of your learners may come with unreasonable expectations about which programme and level are appropriate for them. You will need to be explicit about the entry requirements for their programme;

- identify targets and plan routes towards achieving these; for example, determine your learners' qualification aspirations and explore how these can be achieved;

- enable you to teach your subject in a way that meets different learning styles.

Activity

Make a list of the information you need to know from your learners when they commence with you, to help you teach them effectively.

Your list might contain:

- learner's name, address, telephone number, e-mail;

- any learning difficulty or disability – enabling you to give additional support;

- information regarding dates the learner will be absent;

- previous qualifications and experience;

- preferred learning style.

Programmes aimed at introducing learners to a new subject tend not to require a level of prior knowledge or experience in that subject. For higher level programmes it is essential to ascertain if your learner has the appropriate level of experience and knowledge, along with good literacy, language, numeracy and ICT skills.

It is important to ensure that your learners are on the correct programme, not only for their own benefit, but for your organisation too. You may have retention, achievement and success rate targets set by the Learning and Skills Council (LSC) which can affect the funding your organisation receives.

Conducting an initial assessment of your learners for their chosen programme will ensure they are following the correct route towards achievement.

Different methods of initial assessment

Initial assessment of your learners' skills, knowledge and preferred learning styles should take place before you begin teaching the programme content. This can include the use of a range of tests, questionnaires and interview techniques. You will need to plan what you want to find out from the initial assessment and then choose an appropriate method; for example, an online learning styles questionnaire. Diagnostic tests, for example, a paper-based numeracy or literacy test, can also be carried out. Some learners may be very nervous about taking tests, therefore it is important that the depth and type of initial assessment are appropriate for the programme and the learners.

Example

You are asked to teach 14 learners taking an Access to Nursing programme. They are mainly mature learners who are returning to learning after a career break, many of whom are without any formal qualifications. In the first week, as part of their initial assessment, you ask them to research recent government legislation on health hygiene in hospitals, and to prepare a written paper which covers the implications for the National Health Service. You ask the learners to present their paper at the next session. The following week five learners do not return.

This example demonstrates how important it is to recognise that assessment is a continuous process, starting with a simple initial assessment. If the learners' first experience of assessment terrifies them, they may not return.

Activity

Find out what initial and diagnostic assessments are used in your organisation. Think about the factors that make them effective for learners, teachers and the organisation. You may even think they are not suitable and recommend something different.

Examples of initial and diagnostic assessments may include:

- application/enrolment forms;
- interview/discussion: asking your learner what they want to achieve and discussing their learning history and preferred style of learning;
- observations: it may be necessary to observe your learner in the workplace before agreeing an appropriate programme and level. Observation during induction and initial assessment activities will give you a sense of how your learner performs, which activities they enjoy and which they are least comfortable with;
- self-assessment: asking your learner to assess their own skills and knowledge against the subject. This is often known as a *skills scan*;
- tests; for example, literacy, language, numeracy and ICT. These can be online via the internet or your organisation's intranet;
- structured activities; for example, role play.

If any of your learners do not return to your sessions, this may be as a result of an ineffective induction and initial assessment process. Good practice should have ensured the process helps and supports your learners, before they become a *with-drawal statistic* and thus cause an impact upon your organisation's retention and achievement targets.

Planning and negotiating learning goals

A *learning goal* is what the learner wants to achieve, by attending a relevant pro-gramme of learning with you. The programme will be determined by the qualification content, published by an Awarding or Examining body. You need to know what you are going to teach, and your learners need to know what they are going to learn. These should be formally negotiated and agreed.

> *If you don't know where you are going, it is difficult to select a suitable means for getting there.*
>
> Mager (1984)

A supportive and respectful relationship between your learners and yourself will ensure that realistic goals and targets are agreed, and how their progress will be assessed and recorded.

Learning goals may be categorised as follows:

- overall goals are long-term goals which encompass the whole programme. The aims and objectives/outcomes are usually established either by the organisation or Awarding/Examining body accrediting the programme;
- specific goals are short-term goals which determine changes in the learner's skills, knowledge, understanding and attitudes. The learning process is effective when these goals are clear and match the requirements of the learner;
- immediate goals break down the specific goals into manageable tasks in order that they can be achieved.

Your programme may have an allocation of guided learning hours (GLH) or con-tact/non-contact hours, which is the number of hours within which your learners are expected to achieve the qualification. The hours are sometimes dictated by the Awarding/Examining body and the amount of funding your organisation receives is usually based on these.

You need to ensure that your learners have every opportunity to contribute towards the successful outcome of their learning, by actively involving them in making decisions throughout the programme. This is most effective by setting learning targets, i.e. smaller steps of learning that will help your learners achieve their goals.

Example

Overall goals: *Jane decided to enrol on a six-week Spanish Conversation programme at her local college. At the first session the teacher informed the group about the following:*

- *there would not be a formal examination, assessment would be ongoing;*

- *the aims and objectives of the programme were negotiable with the learners to meet their specific language needs;*

- *the teaching and learning methods to be used.*

The teacher explained that these were planned; however, there was a degree of flexibility to accommodate the learners' interests.

Specific goals: *the teacher proceeded to set out the aims and learning objectives of the first part of the programme, i.e. 'to be able to meet and greet in different situations'. Jane was advised:*

- *what she would be expected to say and write in identified meet-and-greet situations;*

- *the timescale within which she was expected to achieve this.*

The teacher asked if there were any other meet-and-greet situations the group wanted to learn that had not been included in the programme.

Immediate goals: *each week the teacher set out the context, aims and learning objectives for that session. These included:*

- *what Jane would know, be able to say and write by the end of that session;*

- *what activities were planned;*

- *what resources they would be using;*

- *how Jane would be assessed;*

- *a recap and summary;*

- *involvement with the learners to plan the next session.*

By the end of this programme the overall goals will have been achieved, but with negotiation from the learners along the way.

When agreeing targets, these should always be SMART (specific, measurable, achievable, realistic and timebound). This will ensure everyone is clear about what is going to be achieved and why, when, where and how.

Recording learning goals

You should encourage your learners to take ownership of the process of planning their learning journey. To help promote them to become independent learners you will need to negotiate and agree their goals and targets, and assess their progress along the way. It is important that all targets are recorded, whether they are *hard* targets, i.e. directly based on the curriculum, or *soft* targets, i.e. personal and social goals. If you are teaching a programme which does not lead to a formal qualification, you will still need to record learner progress. This is known as *recognising and recording progress and achievement in non-accredited learning* (RARPA).

All relevant information should be recorded in the form of a plan, usually called an *individual learning plan* (ILP) or an action plan. The following is good practice when you are completing an ILP:

- involve your learners, encourage them to discuss their learning and support needs and to use their knowledge of their strengths and areas for development to set their own relevant learning targets;

- refer to the results of initial and diagnostic assessments, and learning styles tests;

- make sure they are individual to each learner, there is no *one size fits all*;

- express and communicate learning targets both verbally and in writing, to enable your learners to understand fully the requirements;

- embed literacy, language, numeracy and ICT goals that are specific, clearly identified, relevant to your learners' needs and to the demands of their programme goals;

- ensure there is a clear link between the learning targets on the ILP, the teaching and learning process, and the qualification aims;

- use regular tutorial and review sessions to update/amend the ILP with your learners.

Activity

Consider whether or not you think your organisation's ILP practice is already well developed or needs improving. If it needs improving, what would you suggest?

You might suggest there is too much paperwork involved and the process could be carried out electronically, or you might want to change the wording on the documents slightly. These changes would help improve the process for both you and your learners.

By now you will have realised that the learner is an individual, and at the centre of your teaching role. If they are on the right programme, with the right support, they should achieve their desired results.

This chapter contributes towards the following minimum core elements (see Appendix 2 for cross-references):

L1, L2, L8, LS1, LS2, LS3, LL1, LR1, LR2, LR3, LW1, LW3;
PLS1, PLS2, PLS3, PLS4, PLR1, PLR2, PLR3, PLL1, PLW1, PLW2, PLW3, PLW4;

N1, N2, N3, NC1, NC2, NP1, NP2, NP3, NP4, NP5, NP6;
PNC1, PNC2, PNC3, PNC4, PNC5, PNP1, PNP2, PNP3, PNP4, PNP5, PNP6,
PNP7, PNP8;
ICT1, ICT2, ICT3, ICT5, ICTC1, ICTC2, ICTP1, ICTP2, ICTP3, ICTPC1, ICTPC2,
ICTPC3, ICTPC4, ICTPC5, ICTPP1, ICTPP2, ICTPP3.

Summary

In this chapter you have learnt about:

- inducting learners;
- icebreaker activities;
- agreeing ground rules with learners;
- the role of initial assessment in the teaching and learning process;
- different methods of initial assessment;
- planning and negotiating learning goals;
- recording learning goals.

References and further information

Daines J W et al (2006) *Adult Learning Adult Teaching* (4th edn), Cardiff: Welsh Academic Press.

DfES (2003) *Success in adult literacy, numeracy and ESOL provision: a guide to support the CIF.*

DfES (2004) *Planning Learning, Recording Progress and Reporting Achievement – a guide for practitioners.*

Knowles MS et al (2005) *The adult learner: the definitive classic in adult education and human resource development*, Oxford: Butterworth-Heinemann/Elsevier.

Mager R F (1984) *Preparing instructional objectives* (2nd edn), Belmont, CA: David S Lake.

Minton D (2005) *Teaching Skills in Further and Adult Education* (3rd edn), Florence, KY: Thomson Learning.

Websites

Adult Learning Inspectorate – www.ali.gov.uk
Education Guardian – www.education.guardian.co.uk
Learning and Skills Network – www.lsneducation.org.uk
Literacy and numeracy online testing – www.move-on.org.uk
Gold Dust Resources – www.goldust.org.uk
Initial Assessment Tools – www.toolslibrary.co.uk

2 PLANNING FOR INCLUSIVE LEARNING

Introduction

In this chapter you will learn about:

- inclusive learning;
- planning and designing learning;
- devising schemes of work;
- devising and adapting session plans;
- learning disabilities and difficulties.

There are activities and examples to help you reflect on the above, which will assist your understanding of how to plan and design inclusive learning to meet the requirements of your learners and the curriculum.

Guidance to address the minimum core of literacy, language, numeracy and information and communication technology (ICT) is integrated throughout and referenced at the end of the chapter.

Chapter 7 contains useful pro formas you may wish to use.

This chapter contributes towards the following: *scope* (S), *knowledge* (K) and *practice* (P) aspects of the professional standards (A–F domains) for teachers, tutors and trainers in the Lifelong Learning Sector:

AS1, AS2, AS3, AS4, AS5, AS6, AS7, AK3.1, AK4.1, AK4.2, AK4.3, AK5.1, AK5.2, AK6.1, AK6.2, AK7.1, AK7.2, AK7.3, AP3.1, AP4.1, AP4.2, AP4.3, AP5.1, AP5.2, AP6.1, AP6.2, AP7.1, AP7.2, AP7.3;
BS1, BS2, BS3, BS4, BK1.1, BK1.2, BK1.3, BK2.1, BK2.2, BK2.3 BK2.4, BK2.5, BK5.1, BK5.2, BP1.1, BP1.2, BP1.3, BP2.1, BP2.2, BP2.3, BP2.4, BP2.5, BP2.6, BP5.1, BP5.2;
CS1, CS3, CS4, CK1.1, CK1.2, CK3.1, CK3.2, CK3.3, CK3.4, CK4.1, CK4.2,
CP1.1, CP1.2, CP3.1, CP3.2, CP3.3, CP3.4, CP4.1, CP4.2;
DS1, DS2, DS3, DK1.1, DK1.2, DK1.3, DK2.1, DK2.2, DK3.1, DK3.2, DP1.1, DP1.2, DP1.3, DP2.1, DP3.1, DP3.2;
EK3.2, EK5.2, EP3.2, EP5.2;
FS1, FS4, FK1.1, FK1.2, FK4.1, FK4.2, FP1.1, FP1.2, FP4.1, FP4.2.

The standards can be accessed at:
http://www.lluk.org.uk/documents/ professional_standards_for_itts_020107.pdf

Inclusive learning

Inclusive learning is about recognising that each of your learners is different from other learners in many ways, and should not be excluded from any activities within your sessions for any legitimate reason. You should plan your teaching and learning sessions to enable all of your learners to take part, and at the end of the programme achieve their learning goals.

> *The aim is not for students to simply take part in further education but to be actively included and fully engaged in their learning. At the heart of our thinking lies the idea of match or fit between how the learner learns best, what they need and want to learn and what is required from the FE sector, the college and teachers for successful learning to take place.*
>
> Tomlinson (1996)

Inclusive learning should ensure a match between the individual learner's requirements and the provision that is made for them. Your organisation may have a *learner entitlement statement* which will reflect learners' individual circumstances and needs. The statement should take into account the needs of particular groups, such as those with learning difficulties or disabilities, a visual or hearing impairment, those whose first language is not English and/or those who require support with their literacy, language, numeracy or ICT skills.

The way in which guidance is given to learners will vary. It should be possible to incorporate some aspects of learners' entitlements and responsibilities in documents such as:

- prospectuses;
- brochures/leaflets;
- existing written statements; for example, learning agreements/contracts;
- training plans/assessment plans;
- induction or enrolment programmes;
- learner charters;
- individual learning plans (ILPs);
- an intranet or website.

As a teacher, you need to work in partnership with your learners to ensure that learning is effective. Partnerships always work best when both sides know where they stand. If your learners understand what is required of them and what they can expect from you, they are more likely to make the necessary commitment to learning and to be successful in achieving their aims and ambitions.

In post-compulsory education there are many challenges in meeting the needs of a wide range of age groups, abilities, subjects and levels.

Activity

Consider how you would promote inclusive learning and equality of opportunity throughout your teaching. How would you give support for and due regard to:

- *any learning difficulties and/or disabilities;*
- *any encounter of harassment or bullying;*
- *literacy and numeracy difficulties?*

When planning your teaching, you should:

- create, design and/or select appropriate resources and activities;
- organise specialist help when needed;
- encourage social, cultural and recreational activities relevant to the programme, if possible;
- provide opportunities for comments and suggestions;
- give honest information about the programme and how it will be organised, taught and assessed;
- signpost/offer guidance towards other learning opportunities.

It is your responsibility to ensure that you provide an inclusive learning environment and equality of opportunity in all aspects of the learning experience.

Planning and designing learning

When you plan and design learning, the five stages of the training cycle should be taken into consideration. These should be followed for teaching and learning to be effective.

Identifying needs and planning

Evaluating

Designing

Assessing

Facilitating

Training cycle

You may have come across the training cycle as part of your *Preparing to Teach in the Lifelong Learning Sector* (PTLLS) programme. The needs of the organisation will be determined by their mission statement, i.e. their purpose, what their aim is, and also by the requirements of their funding providers, if applicable.

Changes in your organisation's priorities may mean changes to the programmes you are teaching. Once the programme and qualification have been confirmed, you will be required to:

- obtain the most recent handbook from the external Awarding/Examining body, which contains details and guidance on procedures, the syllabus and assessment requirements;

- find out if there are professional bodies responsible for identifying and monitoring the standards in your subject area;

- find out what internal quality assurance procedures are in place at your organisation;

- plan the dates and times of delivery for each of your sessions, taking into account public holidays, cultural and religious events, assessment target dates etc;

- find out if there is a dedicated curriculum team of experienced colleagues or staff who can support and help both you and your learners.

You may be teaching a programme that is not an accredited qualification, but you will still be required to find out if there is an existing syllabus or if you need to design your own. If it's the latter, there will probably be organisational requirements for you to follow to ensure you teach your subject correctly. If you are planning and designing the programme yourself, you will need to carry out this process before you begin teaching. Never underestimate how much time this takes, particularly if you are teaching a programme for the first time.

You need to find out what information your organisation collects about your learners before they arrive at the first session and use this to help you plan to meet their requirements.

Example

David enrolled at his local college for a creative arts programme which was to be held in his town's library. When he completed the enrolment form he disclosed that he uses a wheelchair. Unfortunately, when he arrived at the first session, David discovered that the library did not provide access to a disabled toilet.

Sometimes information is not passed on to the teacher from those who have been responsible within the organisation for recruitment and enrolment. This can lead to problems for learners and may even deter some learners from returning. You should be given the relevant information concerning your learners in advance of your first session. This enables you to check that the facilities and resources are suitable. If they are not, you have a chance to contact the learner and discuss any suitable alternatives.

Devising schemes of work

Once you have identified the needs of your organisation and learners, you will plan the teaching and learning process by producing a scheme of work with supporting session plans.

You may be employed as an *associate teacher*, i.e. working from pre-prepared schemes of work and session plans; therefore you are not required to design your own. However, it's a useful skill to be able to plan your own sessions and take control of the content.

The starting point for devising this content will come from an Awarding/Examining body handbook, syllabus, unit specification, or list of learning outcomes/objectives or competences. You will then use this to produce a scheme of work, a logical order of what will be covered during each teaching session. Your scheme of work may include:

- programme information: length, dates, times, Awarding/Examining body details, duration of sessions, venue;

- aims and objectives or learning outcomes/competences broken down into manageable sessions;

- activities and resources;

- assessment and evaluation opportunities.

A rationale will help you when planning your scheme of work, use the WWWWWH (*who, what, when, where, why* and *how*) method.

In your scheme of work the *what* part of the rationale is defined as the programme aims and objectives. Aims are clear and concise statements that describe what you want to achieve. You should decide on the overall programme aims, and also aims for each session, based upon the qualification requirements. However, it may be that you will decide on your own aims in negotiation with your learners if you are designing your own syllabus for a programme without an accredited qualification.

Example

Helga is due to teach a programme for beginners who wish to use the internet. Her overall aim is: to provide an introduction to using the internet.

The aims for her first session are: learners will know and understand all about search engines and e-mail functions.

These aims are rather vague and do not reflect what the learners will actually do. Aims indicate the general direction in which you want to travel but they are not specific enough to tell you *how* to get there or when you have arrived. This is the purpose of objectives or learning outcomes. It is at this point that you are shifting the focus from you as the teacher to your learners. Aims are teacher-centred whereas objectives or learning outcomes are learner-centred. Effective learning outcomes are described as being SMART, i.e. specific, measurable, achievable, realistic and timebound.

Example

Learners will be able to connect to the internet;

Learners will list five search engines;

Learners will use a search engine for a specific purpose;

Learners will explain the advantages and disadvantages of search engines.

You can see that words such as *connect, list, use* and *explain* are SMART and clearly show what the learners will be doing, enabling you as the teacher to observe that learning has taken place. You should be aware when writing your objectives/learning outcomes to include activities that will develop your learners' functional skills of English, maths and ICT. For a comprehensive list of objectives refer to page 27, and Chapter 3 of *Preparing to Teach in the Lifelong Learning Sector* (Gravells, 2008).

It takes a lot of practice to write effective aims, objectives and learning outcomes but you will improve with practice. Be careful not to write these as a list of tasks for *you* to achieve during the session; always consider what the learner will achieve.

When designing your scheme of work, think about the key principles of adult learning based on the work of the American writer Malcolm Knowles (1913–1997). These key principles for successful adult learning are linked to what adults themselves say about their learning. There are six key principles of adult learning:

1 Adults need to know why, what and how they are learning.

2 Their self-concept is important. They often wish to be autonomous and self-directing.

3 Their prior experience is influential. It can be used as a resource for current learning. It can also shape attitudes to current learning.

4 Readiness to learn is important. Adults usually learn best when something is of immediate value.

5 Adults often focus on solving problems in contexts or situations that are important to them.

6 Motivation to learn tends to be based on the intrinsic value of learning and the personal pay-off.

Adults have built up diverse life experiences and knowledge that may include work-related activities, family responsibilities, and previous education. They need to connect their learning to this knowledge or experience. When designing your scheme of work, allow time to incorporate your learners' experiences and knowledge which is relevant to the topic early on in the programme. Relate theories and concepts to the learners and acknowledge the value of their experience throughout their learning. This will give your learners a sense of achievement and desire for more learning.

Depending upon how much time you have to deliver your programme content, you will need to decide what is essential (the *must*), what is important (the *should*) and what is helpful (the *could*). The *product model* ensures all content is delivered within the time, specific only to the qualification. The *process model* adds value to the qualification by teaching other relevant skills and knowledge.

Bloom (1956) believed that education should focus on the *mastery* of subjects and the promotion of higher forms of thinking, rather than an approach which simply transfers facts. Bloom demonstrated decades ago that most teaching tended to be focused on *fact-transfer* and *information recall* (the lowest level of teaching) rather than true meaningful personal development.

Bloom's Taxonomy (1956) model attempts to classify all learning into three parts, or *overlapping domains*:

- *cognitive domain* (intellectual capability, i.e. *knowledge* or *thinking*);

- *affective domain* (feelings, emotions and behaviour, i.e. *attitudes* or *beliefs*);

- *psychomotor domain* (manual and physical skills, i.e. *skills* or *actions*).

The three domains are summarised as knowledge, attitudes and skills, or *think-feel-do*.

In each of the three domains, Bloom's Taxonomy is based on the premise that the categories are ordered in degrees of difficulty. An important premise of Bloom's Taxonomy is that each category (or level) must be mastered before progressing to the next. As such, the categories within each domain are levels of learning development, and these levels increase in difficulty.

Effective learning should cover all the levels of each of the domains, where relevant, to the subject, situation and the learner.

The learner should benefit from the development of knowledge and intellect (*cognitive domain*), attitudes and beliefs (*affective domain*), and the ability to put physical and bodily skills into effect (*psychomotor domain*). The table on page 27 gives some examples of objectives you could use with learners at different levels within these domains.

Although your scheme of work will be formed before you begin teaching, it should be flexible enough to be adapted to respond to the needs of your learners. Once you know more about your learners, you may decide to alter the order in which you've planned your sessions. It may be necessary to allocate more time to one particular session than another depending on your learners' knowledge and experiences.

Cognitive (knowledge)

Entry – recall; repeat;

1 list; recognise; state;

2 compare; describe; identify; select;

3 apply; assess; construct; estimate; explain;

4 illustrate; judge; justify; negotiate; outline; revise; solve; verify;

5 categorise; classify; contrast; criticise; define; evaluate; interpret; organise; review; write;

6 analyse; argue; extrapolate; generalise; summarise; synthesise; translate;

7 accept accountability; critically analyse;

8 display mastery of knowledge; redefine existing procedural knowledge.

Affective (attitudes)

Entry – assume; rely on;

1 adopt; commit; familiarise; co-operate;

2 accept; adapt; develop; express; recognise; understand;

3 appreciate; challenge; defend; determine; discriminate; explain; justify; predict; review; support;

4 command; discuss; generalise; judge; rationalise; react; reflect; watch;

5 argue; define; differentiate; dispute; formulate; suggest; summarise; value;

6 critically discuss; critically reflect; critically review;

7 conduct research; display mastery of complex knowledge;

8 respond to abstract problems.

Psychomotor (skills)

Entry – carry out; receive;

1 adopt; arrange; assemble; attempt; communicate; demonstrate; imitate; show; use;

2 adapt; assist; build; choose; connect; coordinate; create; design; devise; discover; help; perform; rearrange; select;

3 apply; combine; construct; copy; draw; facilitate; make; operate; research;

4 assemble; calculate; diagnose; generate; manipulate; modify; measure; perform;

5 accept responsibility for; establish; manage; modify; teach;

6 transfer and apply; utilise highly specialised skills;

7 demonstrate expertise; display mastery of complex skills; modify advanced skills;

8 lead and initiate complex social processes.

The objectives in this table are a guide only towards each level of the Qualifications and Credit Framework (QCF), you are advised to check your qualification specification requirements.

Example

The initial assessment results from Sonja's Accounts group show that most of her learners have difficulty with percentages. As this is one of the basic calculations required, she has organised a numeracy teacher to deliver a session on percentages, therefore providing a more targeted skills development for her learners.

Your scheme of work should be a working document and you should be prepared to adapt it throughout your teaching.

Activity

Look at a scheme of work you have produced and compare your objectives/outcomes with Bloom's three domains of learning. Which domain and level are you using?

You should always take your learners' abilities into account when devising a scheme of work, ensuring that you can increase these as they progress throughout the programme, to achieve their overall aim.

Devising and adapting session plans

A session plan contains more detail than your scheme of work, and is devised for a particular teaching session, but the two documents should relate to each other. You will find devising and adapting session plans a very time-consuming activity at first, but this does get easier with practice. However, if you are an associate teacher, you may be using session plans devised by others, and you may not be able to amend or deviate from them. Your session plan should be *fit for purpose* in such a way that the learning taking place is set in a realistic context for the programme and/or qualification, whilst meeting the individual needs of your learners. Your learners may have divulged information during induction and initial assessment which will assist you in your planning. For example, you should be aware of their previous learning experiences and any concerns they have about their literacy, language, numeracy or ICT skills. During the first session you could encourage your learners to share information about their interests and hobbies and what their aspirations are. This will help you to get to know your learners, enabling you to individualise learning as necessary. Effective teaching and learning are achieved as a result of careful planning and preparation, and it is your responsibility to ensure that this is completed in plenty of time before teaching your sessions.

Your session plan should include:

● aims and objectives/learning outcomes;

● the context of the session; for example, references to the syllabus/programme being delivered;

- identification of functional skills to be embedded during teaching;

- resources required;

- teaching and learning activities with allocated timings (be prepared to be flexible);

- assessment methods;

- a self-evaluation.

The teaching and learning activities should be matched against your learners' preferred learning styles, and you should identify how much time you will allocate to each. It would be much simpler for you if all your learners were starting from the same point and learned in the same way. However, you should recognise that each learner on your programme will learn in a different way and at a different pace. You will need to be familiar with the range of support and guidance facilities available within your organisation, or externally, and how to access these if necessary. You should therefore use varied activities to reach all learning styles. When planning sessions, consider:

- preferred learning styles, e.g. visual, aural, read/write and kinaesthetic (VARK);

- any support required;

- using practical activities that link to real work experiences, if appropriate;

- inviting guest speakers; for example, past learners who have progressed further, or local employers who can explain job prospects;

- the beginning, middle and end to your session; these should be structured and logical.

See Chapter 3 for a comprehensive list of teaching and learning activities you could use.

At the beginning of your session you should:

- welcome your learners and deal with any notices/changes/updates relating to the programme;

- complete any paperwork; for example, taking the register;

- recap the previous week's learning, ask questions to confirm knowledge and allow time for questions from the learners;

- introduce the aims and objectives/learning outcomes of the session (*what* they will be doing).

Do consider carefully what to deliver in the first part of the session; you need to make an impact to gain and maintain your learners' attention. It may be that some of your learners arrive late due to work commitments. You could plan a *starter activity* to allow for this.

Example

Zarek teaches British Sign Language one evening a week to learners who are at work during the day. The programme is due to start at 6.00 p.m. Due to work commitments, learners arrive at various times during the first 15 minutes of the session. Zarek plans a workshop activity, and speaks to each individual learner about their progress so far. He also encourages learners to ask questions. Once everyone has arrived, he formally commences the session.

This management of time to meet the needs of individual learners can have a positive impact on their progress. Learners will make an effort to arrive as soon as possible if they feel that there is a benefit in doing so.

The main content section will be delivered during the middle section of your session; this is where new facts, knowledge, concepts and skills are taught. Your learners will discover the *why* and *how* of *what* they are expected to be able to do. Your overall aim (*what* you are planning your learners to achieve) will then be broken down into objectives/learning outcomes (*how* the learners will achieve the aim). You should allocate timings to the various teaching and learning activities you plan to use throughout your session. When planning these activities consider the three domains of learning, i.e. cognitive, affective and psychomotor.

It is important to use a variety of strategies when teaching, using visual and verbal stimuli and providing learners with the opportunity to work in large groups, small groups and individually. If they are to work in a personalised way teachers need to know and understand their individual learners, respond to their enthusiasms and interests, and gear assignments towards building on learners' strengths and supporting areas which they find hard.

Duckett and Jones (2006)

It is during the delivery of the main content section of your session that you might adapt your session plan; you need to be flexible to accommodate any changes. While you are teaching, you will find some activities will take longer than you planned, and some will take less time. You might be facilitating a group discussion that you feel is contributing more to learning than you anticipated. You will therefore need to amend your timings of the various activities. You might have some learners who finish an activity before others, so always have a few spare *extension* activities you can use if you need to, rather than leaving learners with nothing to do while others catch up.

You need to decide how you are going to check that learning has taken place, and how you will give feedback to your learners. Assessing your learners' progress should be ongoing and you need to be aware of this throughout the planning process. It is good practice to reinforce learning regularly by linking activities together and asking open questions. Always plan additional activities or materials as a contingency should you have spare time. Additional materials can be used as homework or to extend the learning of those who need further challenges. You should specify additional objectives/learning outcomes for more able learners in your session plan, and how you will support any specific learner needs, for example, dyslexia.

At the end of your session make sure you include a summary of what has been taught. Ensure also that your learners are aware of how to apply their newly acquired skills and knowledge. You can ask some open questions to check knowledge, and give positive praise, encouragement and feedback. It will motivate your learners if you tell them what they will learn in the following session (if applicable). If you are setting any homework, ensure your learners are aware of the requirements. Try to link their learning from one session to the next to enable them to clearly identify their progress.

As soon as possible after the session, you need to carry out a self-evaluation. Make notes of what was achieved, what went particularly well and what didn't. Reflect on and note any changes you would make that would help you if you were to deliver this same session again. Also consider whether or not you need to address any gaps in your own skills and knowledge and identify these in your continuing professional development (CPD) record.

Activity

Look back at your evaluations of sessions you have already delivered. Note in your CPD record any potential training opportunities you have identified.

It's crucial to prepare your session plan well, to enable effective teaching and learning to take place.

To fail to plan is to plan to fail.

G Petty (2004)

Learning disabilities and difficulties

From Exclusion to Inclusion, the report of the Disability Rights Task Force (December 1999), estimates that at least 8.5 million people currently meet the Disability Discrimination Act (1995) definition of disability. It also states that disabled people are twice as likely as non-disabled people to be unemployed and to have no formal qualifications. People who have disabilities and learning difficulties play an important role in all aspects of life. If Britain is to fulfil its aim of being a fully inclusive society, everyone should be able to fulfil his or her potential and gain the skills to participate and contribute.

Your learners will gain confidence in their own ability to learn if they are taught in a way that suits them. While teaching learners according to their learning style has been shown to benefit all learners, it becomes essential for your learners with learning difficulties and disabilities, as they may be able to use only some styles of learning. Planning to use teaching and learning activities that suit your learners is an effective way of creating a successful learning experience, and counteracting any previous failures. Offering your learners opportunities to learn in the way that best suits them is the essence of inclusive learning.

Some disabilities such as dyslexia may be partially defined by the learning style. Dyslexic learners are often weak in *left-brained* language, logic and sequence, so may rely on *right-brained* approaches such as using their imagination and visual representations.

At some point, your learners may need some extra help with learning. Some will have specific learning difficulties relating to language learning and skill development. These may include dyslexia and dyspraxia but others may have a general cognitive learning difficulty which affects their ability to learn. The following are some of the conditions you may encounter:

- dyslexia – difficulty with processing written language;

- dyspraxia – poor motor co-ordination or clumsiness;

- dysgraphia – difficulty with handwriting;

- autistic spectrum disorder, Asperger's syndrome – difficulty with social interaction and with abstract concepts;

- dyscalculia – difficulty with calculations or maths.

- attention deficit hyperactivity disorder (ADHD) – a common behavioural disorder. Learners have difficulty controlling their behaviour without medication or behavioural therapy. Although not diagnosed as a learning difficulty, its interference with concentration and attention can make it difficult for a learner to perform well.

Example

Stuart has been diagnosed with Asperger's syndrome and is attending a plumbing apprenticeship course at his local college. He has difficulties in understanding the social and cultural 'rules' that most people take for granted, and so misinterprets intentions, behaviour and the conversation of others. On the surface; Stuart appears to be rude and disruptive and constantly interrupts when others are speaking. His teacher is aware of this, and Stuart and the group have discussed ways of dealing with situations as they arise.

It's important that you are aware of any learning difficulties or disabilities in order to support your learners fully. Initial assessment should have identified these; however, sometimes learners may talk to you in confidence about their concerns or requirements. If you are unsure how to help, just ask your learners what you can do; they are best able to explain how you can help make their learning experience a positive one.

Technological advances have made an enormous difference to learners who have learning difficulties and disabilities, enabling them to access suitable learning opportunities. This is particularly true for learners who have physical or sensory impairments and also for those who are dyslexic or have other learning difficulties. *Assistive and enabling technology* provides a means of access to learning for those who:

- are blind or partially sighted;

- are dyslexic;

- have a degenerative condition which is tiring;

- are deaf or have partial hearing;

- have difficulty with manipulation and fine motor control;

- have difficulty in speaking.

Efficient use of technology relies on carrying out detailed and effective initial assessment, followed up by reviews with learners at appropriate stages in their progress. It also requires human resources in the form of technicians and competent support workers to train teachers and learners to use the technology. The management of such staff is an essential part of planning learning programmes. However, technology is not a universal remedy for all learners.

You may be asked to teach learners who have a wide range of difficulties or disabilities. Having an individual learning plan for each will help you meet their needs, while ensuring that you achieve the aims of the programme.

Activity

Ask at your organisation if they have a policy to provide access to assistive technology in order to support learners with disabilities or learning difficulties. You need to know what is available and how to use it. You should also be aware of any relevant legislation.

There might be specialist staff in your organisation to assist learners requiring support. Your session plan should list any support staff required and how they will be used to assist your learners.

The provision of learning opportunities is not just a matter for individual teachers but requires a whole organisation approach to create an appropriate and effective learning environment.

This chapter contributes towards the following minimum core elements (see Appendix 2 for cross-references):

L1, L2, L3, L4, L8, LS1, LS2, LS3, LL1, LR1, LR2, LR3, LW1, LW3;
PLS1, PLS2, PLS3, PLS4, PLL1, PLR1, PLR2, PLR3, PLW1, PLW2, PLW3, PLW4;
N1, N2, N3, N4, N5, NC1, NC2, NP1, NP2, NP3, NP4, NP5, NP6;
PNC1, PNC2, PNC3, PNC4, PNC5, PNP1, PNP2, PNP3, PNP4, PNP5, PNP6, PNP7, PNP8;
ICT1, ICT2, ICT3, ICT4, ICT5, ICTPC1, ICTPC4, ICTPP1, ICTPP2, ICTPP3.

Summary

In this chapter you have learnt about:

- inclusive learning;

- planning and designing learning;

- devising schemes of work;

- devising and adapting session plans;

- learning disabilities and difficulties.

References and further information

Bloom B S (ed.) (1956) *Taxonomy of Educational Objectives, the classification of educational goals – Handbook I: Cognitive Domain*, New York: McKay.

Daines J W et al (2006) *Adult Learning Adult Teaching* (4th edn), Cardiff: Welsh Academic Press.

Disability Rights Task Force (1999) *From Exclusion to Inclusion*, London: DRTF.

Duckett I, and Jones C A (2006) *Personalised learning: meeting individual learner needs*, London: Learning and Skills Network.

Gravells Ann (2008) *Preparing to Teach in the Lifelong Learning Sector* (3rd edn), Exeter: Learning Matters.

Knowles M S (1990) *The adult learner: a neglected species*, Houston: Gulf Publishing.

Learning and Skills Council (2001) *Learners' Entitlement*.

Minton D (2005) *Teaching Skills in Further and Adult Education* (3rd edn), Florence, KY: Thomson Learning.

Petty G (2004) *Teaching Today*, Cheltenham: Nelson Thornes.

Tomlinson M (1996) *Inclusive Learning*, Further Education Funding Council Learning Difficulties and/or Disabilities.

Websites

Access for all – http://www.dfes.gov.uk/curriculum_literacy/

Bloom's Taxonomy – http://www.businessballs.com/bloomstaxonomyoflearning domains.htm

Disability Discrimination Act – http://www.opsi.gov.uk/Acts/acts2005/ukpga_20050013_en_1

Equality and Human Rights Commission – http://www.uk250.co.uk/frame/4060/disability-rights-commission.html

Goldust Resources – www.goldust.org.uk

Learning Styles – www.vark-learn.com

3 TEACHING AND LEARNING STRATEGIES

Introduction

In this chapter you will learn about:

- teaching and learning;

- integrating literacy, language, numeracy and ICT skills within the teaching context;

- assessment;

- feedback;

- quality assurance.

There are activities and examples to help you reflect on the above, which will assist your understanding of how to teach effectively. Appendix 3 contains useful tips for teaching.

Guidance to address the minimum core of literacy, language, numeracy and information and communication technology (ICT) is integrated throughout and referenced at the end of the chapter.

Chapter 7 contains useful pro formas you may wish to use.

This chapter contributes towards the following: *scope* (S), *knowledge* (K) and *practice* (P) aspects of the professional standards (A–F domains) for teachers, tutors and trainers in the Lifelong Learning Sector.

AS1, AS2, AS3, AS5, AS6, AS7, AK2.1, AK2.2, AK3.1, AK4.1, AK4.2, AK4.3, AK5.1, AK5.2, AK7.2, AK7.3, AP1.1, AP2.1, AP2.2, AP3.1, AP4.1, AP5.1, AP5.2, AP6.1, AP6.2, AP7.1, AP7.2, AP7.3;
BS1, BS2, BS3, BS4, BS5, BK1.1, BK1.2, BK2.1, BK2.3, BK2.4, BK2.5, BK2.6, BK2.7, BK3.1, BK3.2, BK3.3, BK3.5, BK4.1, BP1.1, BP1.2, BP1.3, BP2.1, BP2.2, BP2.3, BP2.4, BP2.5, BP2.6, BP2.7, BP3.1, BP3.2, BP3.3, BP3.4, BP3.5, BP4.1;
CS1, CS4, CK2.1, CK3.1, CK3.3, CK3.5, CP1.1, CP1.2, CP2.1, CP3.1, CP3.2, CP3.5, CP4.2;
DS1, DS3, DK3.2, DP1.2, DP2.1, DP3.1, DP3.2;
ES1, ES2, ES3, ES4, ES5, EK1.1, EK1.2, EK1.3, EK2.1, EK2.2, EK2.3, EK2.4, EK3.1, EK3.2, EK4.1, EK4.2, EK5.1, EK5.2, EK5.3, EP1.1, EP1.2, EP1.3, EP2.1, EP2.2, EP2.4, EP3.1, EP3.2, EP4.1, E4.2, EP5.1, EP5.2, EP5.5;
FK4.2, FP1.2, FP2.1, FP4.2.

The standards can be accessed at: http://www.lluk.org.uk/documents/professional_standards_for_itts_020107.pdf

Teaching and learning

There are many different strategies and methods of teaching and learning. Depending upon the subject you are teaching, you need to choose methods which are appropriate to the topic, subject level and abilities of your learners. You should also take into account the environment you are teaching in, the resources available to you and any prior knowledge and experience of your learners. Once you know which subject or qualification you will be teaching, you need to decide upon the approach you will take. Will you be teaching formally, for example, giving a lecture; or informally, for example, facilitating group discussions?

John Dewey (1859–1952) believed that formal schooling was falling short of its potential. He emphasised facilitating learning through promoting various activities rather than by using a traditional teacher-focused method. He believed that children learned more from guided experience than from authoritarian instruction. He subscribed to a *learner-focused* philosophy and argued that *learning is life*, not just *preparation for* life. This is also applicable to adult learners. Using different teaching methods, combined with learner activities, will help reach the different learning styles of the individuals you are teaching. Fleming (1987) categorised learning styles as *visual (seeing)*, *aural (hearing)* and *kinaesthetic (doing)*.

Activity

Carry out a search via the internet for learning styles, or ask in your organisation which learning styles tests they recommend. Compare different theorists and styles. You could try taking a test yourself to see what your learning style is, or if you have taken one before, to see if you have changed.

Knowing your own learning style, and that of your learners, will help you plan which teaching and learning methods are best suited to your learners. Laird (1985) suggests that learning occurs when the senses of *sight*, *hearing*, *touch*, *smell* and *taste* are stimulated. This is easy if you are teaching a practical session, but not so if you are teaching a theoretical subject. However, if you are willing to try something different, you can make your sessions really interesting and memorable, but don't drop an apple on a learner's head to demonstrate the law of gravity! Whenever possible, link theory to practice, and use practical activities based around the subject and the areas of interest of your learners. If you can make your session fun and interesting, relating to all the senses, it will help your learners remember the topics better. Don't forget two other senses you can use as a teacher: a sense of humour and common sense.

There are many theories regarding learning; unfortunately, there is not enough room in this book to explore them all. If you have time, read other relevant textbooks for further information or carry out a search via the internet for *theories of learning*.

Formal teaching is known as *pedagogy*, where the teacher directs all the learning. This method does not allow for individual learning styles to be taken into account. Teaching methods which focus on the learner are known as *andragogy*; for example, group work and discussions. Malcolm Knowles (2005) initially defined andragogy as *the art and science of helping adults learn*. An andragogical approach places more emphasis on what the learner is doing. Try and maximise the use of your learners' experiences by involving them whenever possible. Learners can learn from their peers' knowledge and experiences, as well as from you.

Example

Patrick teaches history. In the past he has used a pedagogical approach by introducing the topics, explaining them to his learners and dictating important dates and facts. He wants to include his learners more by taking an andragogical approach. He has chosen to do this by introducing the topic, then facilitating a group discussion based around the learners' prior knowledge. He uses a computerised presentation to display relevant dates and facts, supported with pictures and links to video clips via the internet. A quiz is then used to test the learners' knowledge. If there is time, Patrick uses role play, enabling the learners to act out historical events. He always asks open questions and involves all his learners, using their names. This andragogical approach therefore reaches all learning styles and ensures the session is interesting and active.

When teaching, you should always refer to your session plan, be organised and professional, and follow all relevant policies, procedures and codes of practice. Careful planning and preparation will lead to an effectively delivered session, with all learners having learned what you intended them to learn.

Activity

Plan a one-hour session based upon your specialist subject, which combines several teaching methods and learner activities. Use your imagination to bring your subject to life, thereby making your session memorable to your learners. Refer to the table on pages 38–48 for some ideas and use the session plan pro forma in chapter 7.

Experimenting with new or different teaching methods and activities will make your sessions interesting and should reach all learning styles. Do keep focused upon your topic and the timings. If a particular activity is going well, you could let this run over time, and reduce the time for other activities. If you have spare time at the end, ask each learner in turn to state *one thing* they have learned during the session.

What really matters is what is being *learnt*; when choosing appropriate teaching methods, ensure you keep this in mind.

The following table lists some ideas for teaching and learning activities that you could use, with a brief description, and the advantages and disadvantages of each. When using activities, you need to ensure that they are inclusive, and that they differentiate for individual learning styles and needs, learner difficulties and/or disabilities. Always follow health and safety guidelines, and carry out any relevant risk assessments. Make sure your learners are aware of *why* they are carrying out the activities and don't overcomplicate your sessions.

Method	Description	Advantages	Disadvantages
Activities	Tasks carried out by a group or individual, relevant to the topic being taught	Learners are active Develops group interaction	Not all learners may want to participate Clear objectives should be set, activity must be clearly explained Time limit required Time needed for feedback or debrief
Assignments	A longer-term activity based around the qualification or topic, which provides evidence of learning Can be practical or theoretical	Can be produced by the teacher to challenge a learner's potential or consolidate learning Can be formative or summative	If set by an Awarding/Examining body, need to ensure all aspects of the syllabus have been taught beforehand Must be individually assessed, and written feedback given which can develop learning further
Blended learning	Using more than one method of teaching, usually including technology. For example, a teaching session can be supported with learning materials and resources available via the organisation's website, with e-support/assessment from teachers as required	Several methods of learning can be combined, enabling all learning styles to be met Formal teaching can be supported with informal learning	Not all learners may have access to the technology
Buzz groups	Short topics to be discussed in small groups	Can break up a more formal session Allows interaction of learners and focuses ideas Checks understanding Doesn't require formal feedback	Learners may digress Specific points could be lost Checking individual learning has taken place may be difficult

	Description		
Case studies	Can be a hypothetical situation, a description of an actual event or an incomplete event, enabling learners to write about how they would deal with it	Can make topics more realistic, enhancing motivation and interest Can be carried out individually or in a group situation Builds on current knowledge and experience	Time limits must be set If carried out as a group activity, roles should be defined Must have clear outcomes Allow time for a debrief to include a group discussion
Coaching	A one-to-one, or small group activity which involves the teacher giving a demonstration. This is then followed by an observation of the learner's performance	Ideal for on-the-job training Ongoing advice and guidance can be given Takes account of individual needs	Not suitable for large groups Can be time-consuming Suitable environment needed
Debates	Knowledgeable group members or guests present a case to the learners, with subsequent arguments, questions and discussions	Learner-centred Allows freedom of viewpoints	Some learners may not get involved, others may take over – teacher needs to manage this carefully Can be time-consuming Learners may need to research a topic in advance
Demonstration	A practical way of showing how something works	Can be supported with handouts and activities to cover all learning styles Can increase attention and confidence	Equipment may not be available or in working order Larger groups may not be able to see the demonstration Individuals may not pay attention or may get bored
Dictation	Reading notes out loud for learners to write down	Gives emphasis to key points – in moderation	Learners write down what is said, but may not understand it Some learners may get behind with their writing and miss points Does not allow for clarification or questions

Method	Description	Advantages	Disadvantages
Discussion	Learners talk about a topic or the teacher can introduce a topic for the group to discuss	All learners can participate Useful for affective domain objectives	Some learners may be shy or not want to be involved Easy to digress Teacher needs to keep the group focused and set a time limit
Distance learning	Learning which takes place away from the organisation offering the programme/qualification Work can be posted to learners and returned for assessment	Learning can occur at a time and place to suit the learner	Could be a long gap between returning work for assessment and receiving feedback Self-discipline is needed Targets must be clearly agreed Learner may never meet teacher/assessor
Drawing	Illustrations to show how something works	Good for visual learners	Needs to be carefully explained
e-learning (see also online learning)	*Electronic learning* – learning which is supported or enhanced using information and communication technology (ICT)	Learning can take place anywhere a computer is available Learning can be flexible Ongoing support is given	Learners need access to a computer and need to be computer literate Self-discipline is needed, along with clear targets Authenticity of learner's work may need to be validated Technical support may be required
Essays	A formal piece of written text, produced by the learner, for a specific topic	Useful for academic subjects Can check a learner's language and literacy skills	Not suitable for lower level learners Marking can be time-consuming Plagiarism can be an issue
Experiential tasks	Practical tasks enabling learners to act out or experience an event	Good for group work and to put theory into practice Learners find out things for themselves	Not all learners may want to participate Can be time-consuming

Flexible learning	Learning that can take place at a time and place to suit the learner and/or using different learning methods	Suits learners who cannot attend formal sessions	Ongoing support and monitoring of achievement is required Not all learners are motivated to this style of learning
Games	A fun way of learning in pairs or groups to enable problem-solving and decision-making to take place	Board or card games can be designed to make learning enjoyable Tests knowledge Physical games put theory into practice Encourages interaction and healthy competition	Need to be well prepared in advance Learners need to remain focused Objectives need to be clear A *pilot* should take place first to make sure it works Careful supervision is needed Rules must be followed
Group work	Enables learners to carry out a specific activity, for example, problem solving Can be practical or theoretical	Allows interaction between learners Learners learn from each other Encourages participation and variety Rotating group members enables all learners to work with each other	Careful management by the teacher is required regarding time limits, progress, and ensuring all group members are clear about the requirements Could be personality problems with team members or large groups One person may dominate Time is needed for a thorough debrief and feedback
Handouts	Written information/drawings etc to promote and support learning	Useful for learners to refer to after a session Can incorporate questions for learners to answer as a homework activity Can be differentiated for levels of learners	Should be used in conjunction with other activities Needs to be adapted for any special learner requirements Should be produced well in advance Spelling, grammar, punctuation and syntax must be accurate
Homework	Activities carried out between sessions, for example, further reading, answering questions	Learners can complete at a time and place that suits them Maintains interest between sessions Encourages learners to stretch themselves further	Clear time limits must be set Learners might not do it Must be discussed, or marked/assessed and individual feedback given

Method	Description	Advantages	Disadvantages
Icebreakers/team-building exercises	A fun and lighthearted way of introducing learners and topics	A good way of learners getting to know each other, and for teachers to observe skills and attitudes Can revitalise a flagging session	Not all learners may want to take part Some learners may see these as insignificant — careful explanations are needed to link the experience to the topic
Instruction	Formal method of teaching learners, whereby the teacher tells or shows the learner what to do, to achieve a particular skill; the learner then performs this	If one-to-one, a good method of pacing learning to suit the individual Learners can hear and/or see what they should do, and try this out immediately	If to a group, some learners may get left behind or forget what to do Needs to be supported with a handout or further information/activities Appropriate positioning is required; for example for left-handed learners of right-handed teachers
Interviews	Practical activity to demonstrate skills and knowledge of a particular topic, for example, applying for a job	Gives learners the opportunity to demonstrate communication skills Learners can observe different interviews and give peer feedback	Needs to be managed carefully Not all learners may want to take part Clear roles and boundaries should be defined Time limit should be set
Journal or diary	Learners keep a record of their progress, their reflections and thoughts	Develops self-assessment skills Relates theory to practice (if learners are having work experience) Helps the teacher assess language and literacy skills	Should be specific to the learning taking place and be analytical rather than descriptive Contents need to remain confidential Can be time-consuming to read
Lecture	Traditional teacher-centred technique of delivering information	Useful for teaching theoretical subjects Key points can be prepared in advance on postcards, as prompts Ideal for large groups Can be supported with visual images	Learners are passive and may not listen to what is being said Learners may not feel they can ask questions to clarify points Learners need good listening and note-taking skills Good voice projection and clarity of speech required

Strategy	Description	Advantages	Disadvantages/considerations
Mentoring	One-to-one guidance and support by someone other than the teacher, who is experienced in the subject	Expertise and knowledge can be passed on through ongoing support Times can be arranged to suit both parties	Can be time-consuming Mentor and mentee might not get along
Micro-teaching	A session taught by the learner, usually in front of their peer group	Enables learners to practise in a safe environment Can be recorded to aid self-evaluation Peer feedback can be given by the other learners	Not all learners enjoy the experience Recording equipment can be difficult to manage while observing learners Some learners may not give constructive feedback
Mind maps/spidergrams	A visual way of organising information and making plans. Learners draw a circle with a key point and branch from this with subheadings to explore and develop points further	Learners are active Topics can be explored in a fun and meaningful way Links between ideas are easy to see New information can easily be added	Not all learners may want to contribute One learner may dominate Needs careful supervision Large paper or a board and marker pens required
Models	Useful where the real object cannot be seen Life models, for example, in art classes	Learners have a chance to see how something looks and/or works, and ask questions	Must be clearly explained and demonstrated Needs careful planning and preparation Should be supported with a handout
Online learning (see also e-learning)	Learning that takes place in a Virtual Learning Environment (VLE) via a computer connected to an intranet or the internet Asynchronous learning does not need to be accessed at fixed times Synchronous learning takes place in an environment where the teacher and learner are simultaneously present, perhaps at different locations, but communicating with each other in real time	Learning can take place anywhere a computer with internet access is available Learning can be flexible Ongoing support is given	Learners need access to a computer with internet access Learners need to be computer literate Self-discipline is needed, along with clear targets Authenticity of learner's work may need to be validated Technical support may be required Reliable internet connection needed

Method	Description	Advantages	Disadvantages
Peer learning/ feedback	Learners gaining skills and/or knowledge from their peers	Enables learners to work together in an informal way to learn from each other's experiences and knowledge Learners support each other throughout the session or programme Learners give feedback after their peers carry out a task	There may be personality clashes resulting in subjective feedback Not all information given may be correct
Practical work	A task that individuals can carry out while the teacher observes progress; usually follows a demonstration or presentation	Actively involves the learners Help and advice can be given as needed	Some learners may not respond well to practical activities Can be time-consuming
Presentations	Similar to a lecture, with greater use of audio-visual aids	Interaction can take place between the teacher and learners Visual and aural learning styles can be reached	Kinaesthetic learning styles might not be included Some learners may not pay attention Too many slides can switch off learners' attention
Projects	A longer-term activity enabling learners to provide evidence of, or consolidate, their learning	Can be interesting and motivating Can be individual or group led Learners could choose a relevant topic to cover the learning outcomes, leading to autonomous learning	Clear outcomes must be set, along with a time limit, and must be relevant, realistic and achievable Progress should be checked regularly If a group is carrying out the project, ensure that you are aware of each individual's input Thorough feedback should be given
Questions	A key technique for checking understanding and stimulating thinking	Can be written or verbal Enable the learner to think about what they are learning Can challenge a learner's potential An effective way of testing knowledge when open questions are used	Closed questions elicit only a Yes or No response which doesn't demonstrate knowledge Questions must be unambiguous

Quizzes	Fun activities to test knowledge, skills and/or attitudes by the use of crosswords, panel games etc	Learners are actively involved Useful backup activity if you have spare time	Can seem trivial to mature learners
Reading	Learners work from relevant texts/books/ journals etc	Good for *read/write* learning styles Encourages further learning	Reading and note-taking skills required Learners can get bored or easily distracted May need to have differentiated texts to account for a range of levels in the group
Reports	Learners produce a document to inform, recommend and/or make suggestions based on a given topic	Useful for higher level learners Encourages the use of research techniques	Learners need research and academic writing skills Learners need to interpret and evaluate their reading to demonstrate their understanding
Research	An in-depth way of finding out answers or more information about a topic	Learners can use the internet, texts, journals etc in their own time	Learners need academic writing skills; for example, the use of *Harvard* referencing
Role plays	Acting out a hypothetical situation	Enables you to see learners' behaviour Encourages participation A fun method of learning Can lead to debates Links theory to practice	Can be time-consuming Clear roles must be defined Not all learners may want, or be able, to participate Some learners may get too dramatic Time needed for a thorough debrief
Seminars	A presentation of ideas, followed by questions and a discussion – usually by the learners	Allows learners to research topics and gain confidence in speaking to a group Can lead to worthwhile discussions	Need to agree topics well in advance as well as running order of who will present first Learners need specific objectives and a time limit Other learners may not pay attention

Method	Description	Advantages	Disadvantages
Simulation	An imitation activity carried out when the real activity would be too dangerous. For example, the evacuation of a building when the fire alarm goes off; you don't have to set fire to the building for a simulated evacuation	Enables learners to demonstrate skills Learners may realise things about themselves they were not aware of	Careful planning is needed Can be time-consuming Specialist equipment may be needed Ground rules must be agreed Not all learners may be able to participate fully May not be taken seriously Thorough debrief needed
Surveys	Learners ascertain information regarding a particular topic, from others	Active task; learners can work individually, in pairs or in groups Learners can meet other people, enhancing their experience	Permission may be required Ethics and confidentiality required Confidentiality should be maintained Time-consuming to mark and validate
Teaching/training/ tutoring	Educating learners in a subject, furthering their knowledge, skills and/or attitudes	A variety of methods can be used depending upon the subject If planned well, can reach all learning styles, motivate learners and encourage development and progression	Some learners do not respond well to formal teaching Not all learning styles reached all of the time
Team-teaching	Facilitating a session with a colleague	Enables learners to see different styles of delivery	Staff involved need to plan carefully who is doing what and when
Technology-based learning	Using relevant equipment and materials, for example, videos/CD-ROMs/DVDs/the internet etc	Generates discussions and leads to further learning Brings *real* events to learners Films can be repeated or paused if necessary for questions	Can be time-consuming Learners need to pay attention Learners should not be left unsupervised
Tests	Written questions (open, closed, multiple choice) to test knowledge Practical activities to assess skills	Learners are active Can be used to fill in time towards the end of a session or to extend learning Useful for individual learners who like to be challenged further	Needs to be carried out in supervised conditions Time limits required Can be stressful to learners Feedback may not be immediate If set by an Awarding/Examining body, need to ensure all aspects of the syllabus have been taught before issuing the test

Tutorials	A one-to-one or group discussion between the teacher and the learner(s), with an agreed purpose; for example, discussing progress so far	A good way of informally assessing a learner's progress and/or giving feedback An opportunity for learners to discuss issues or for informal tuition to take place	Needs to be in a comfortable, safe and quiet environment as confidential issues may be discussed Time may overrun Records should be maintained and action points followed up
Undoing	Learners can *undo* or *take apart* an object, to learn how it was put together. An example is taking a plug apart to see how it was wired	Great for kinaesthetic learners Needs to be demonstrated by the teacher first Useful in practical sessions, needs to be supported with a handout and careful guidance	Not so good for theoretical learners Objects/resources need to be available for all learners
Visiting speakers	An expert in the subject area speaks to the group	Can give variety and expertise to a topic, with a different perspective	Must be arranged well in advance Some speakers may charge a fee Need to allow time for questions and discussions
Visits/field trips	Learners visit a venue relevant to the programme or qualification	Fact-finding, active, interesting and stimulating Makes the subject real Puts theory into practice Can be discussed in subsequent sessions Can link with projects and assignments	Needs careful planning, organisational and health & safety procedures must be followed Needs finance Group needs to be well briefed and prepared, ground rules must be set Supervision usually required Debrief needed
Word shower (also known as brainstorming)	A list of suggestions or ideas regarding a particular theme, topic or problem without judgements or criticisms The list can then be refined and used as a basis for other activities, usually written on flipchart paper or a board so all learners can see	Quickly stimulates thoughts and ideas Involves everyone Builds on current knowledge and experience Can be teacher led or group led	Some learners may not contribute Ideas may be given too quickly to write down Time limits need to be set

Method	Description	Advantages	Disadvantages
Worksheets	Interactive handouts to check knowledge (can also be electronic) Blank spaces can be used for learners to complete sentences Words can be circled, phrases completed, lists sorted etc	Fun, informal activity, can be done individually, in pairs or groups Useful for lower level learners or homework Can be created at different degrees of difficulty to address differentiation	Mature learners may consider them inappropriate Too many worksheets can be boring, learners might not be challenged enough
Workshops	Practical or simulated activities in a realistic environment	Enable learners to work at their own pace Learners can support each other and learn from each other's experiences	Individual support is required Suitable workpacks need to be produced or resource packs need to be purchased to enable learners to progress at their own pace

Integrating literacy, language, numeracy and ICT skills within the teaching context

As a teacher, you should be able to demonstrate your own competence in the areas of literacy, language, numeracy and ICT; these are known as the *minimum core*.

Improving your skills in these areas will enable you to consider how best to teach your subject in ways that support the development of your learners' skills. It is important for you to acknowledge that literacy, language, numeracy and ICT are crucial for the achievement of your learners' qualification. Some learners may not have adequate skills in reading, writing, working with numbers and/or using a computer; developing these skills in your learners can bring positive results.

You need to ensure that your own personal skills are adequate in order to help develop those of your learners. For example, you might encourage your learners to use the internet as a research tool, but not feel very confident using it yourself.

Activity

Look at Appendix 2 – Summary of minimum core elements – and see which ones you feel competent to do. You could complete the personal development plan in Chapter 7 for any training needs you feel you have identified.

Integrating literacy, language, numeracy and ICT into your sessions is part of your professional role as a teacher. If you are not competent in these skills yourself, you may be making errors but not realise this. When planning your sessions, consider which aspects of these skills you want your learners to demonstrate within the context of their subject; for example, the use of literacy and language when they are reading and writing. Then, when marking their work, ensure that you comment on any errors of spelling, grammar and punctuation to help your learners improve.

You may be familiar with the terms *skills for life, basic skills, core skills, key skills* and *functional skills* which have been referred to in the past. These are all aimed at ensuring that learners have the skills required to work confidently, effectively and independently in life and work.

If you took the Preparing to Teach in the Lifelong Learning Sector qualification, you would have embedded *functional skills* within your teaching. These skills are maths, English and ICT. You might not be an expert in these, but improving your own skills in the minimum core will help. However, you need to recognise when your learners might require further support that you don't feel confident to give, and will there-fore need to liaise with other specialist teachers at your organisation.

When teaching, you should ensure that your learners are aware of how these skills relate to their learning.

Example

Owen is a cookery teacher and is due to teach a session about healthy eating. He wants to encourage his learners to use their maths, English and ICT skills. His learners will therefore research and read recipes using cookery magazines, books and the internet, write shopping lists, communicate with others, buy the ingredients, word process a menu and then cook the meal. Owen will ensure his learners use the correct amounts of ingredients required by working these out in both metric and imperial measures. They will also calculate portion sizes and the cost of ingredients, along with the calorie content for each meal cooked. Owen has therefore successfully embedded all functional skills as part of his session.

In the above example, everyday aspects of functioning, based upon the subject were integrated during the session. The learners' skills should improve by the application of their knowledge within the subject.

Some examples of integrating the skills into your delivery are:

- literacy – reading, writing, spelling, grammar, punctuation, syntax;
- language – speaking, listening, role play, interviews;
- numeracy – calculations, interpretations, evaluations, measurements;
- ICT – online learning, e-learning, word processing, use of a virtual learning environment (VLE), e-mails.

As a teacher, you can play an important part in providing opportunities to develop your learners' skills of literacy, language, numeracy and ICT. It is your responsibility to continually update your own skills in these areas by undertaking professional development; improving yourself will help improve your learners.

Assessment

Assessment is a measure of learning, at a given point in time. Relevant skills, knowledge and/or attitudes can be measured towards a subject or qualification. As a teacher, you need to know how well your learners are progressing, and to plan further training and assessment as necessary.

There are several methods of assessment, some of these formal – for example, observations, tests and examinations – and some informal, for example, oral questioning or quizzes. There are also assessment types such as *initial* (at the beginning), *formative* (ongoing) and *summative* (at the end). You will need to look at the syllabus or qualification handbook for your subject, for guidance regarding the methods and types of assessment you will need to use.

Assessment planning should be specific, measurable, achievable, realistic and time bound (SMART):

- Specific – the activity relates only to the standards/learning outcomes being assessed and is clearly stated;

- Measurable – the activity can be measured against the standards/learning outcomes, allowing gaps to be identified;

- Achievable – the activity can be achieved at the right level;

- Realistic – the activity is relevant and will give consistent results;

- Timebound – target dates/times for each activity are agreed by the teacher and learner.

When planning for assessment, always consider *who, what, when, where, why* and *how*. This should ensure that you take into account all the relevant aspects to assess your learners successfully.

Some assessment materials may be provided for you; for example, assignments which are set externally by the Awarding/Examining body. If these are not provided, you will need to produce your own assessment activities, along with marking criteria to ensure you are assessing fairly.

Activity

Acquire a syllabus for your specialist subject. These can be located via the relevant Awarding/Examining body's websites, or ask in your organisation. Look at the assessment criteria; do you feel these methods would be fair to all your learners? Do you need to produce sample answers or are these supplied for you? What documentation do you need to complete to prove that your learners have achieved the required outcomes?

You need to keep records of assessment, to satisfy your organisation, relevant external agencies and the Awarding/Examining body. If you are assessing a National Vocational Qualification (NVQ), you should prepare an assessment plan in advance, based on the relevant assessment criteria, assess appropriately and give feedback. If you are marking work or setting tests, you will need to do this fairly and give feedback to your learners, keeping records of their achievements.

Example

Serena has been assessing the NVQ in Motor Vehicle Maintenance and is due to be visited by the Awarding body's external verifier. Serena has an internal verifier within her organisation who has sampled her assessment decisions, observed her assessment practice and talked to some of her learners. Serena has prepared for this visit by ensuring she has a file of all her original records relating to assessment planning, reviews and feedback, along with learner portfolios of evidence, and her internal verifier's records. The external verifier will sample some of her records, along with the learners' portfolios to ensure that Serena is complying with the Awarding body's requirements.

All work assessed should be valid, authentic, current, sufficient and reliable (VACSR):

- valid – the work is relevant to the standards/criteria being assessed;
- authentic – the work has been produced solely by the learner;
- current – the work is still relevant at the time of assessment;
- sufficient – the work covers all the standards/criteria;
- reliable – the work is consistent across all learners, over time and at the required level.

Feedback

This can be carried out formally after an assessment, or informally during a teaching session, review or tutorial. All learners need to know how they are progressing; this will help to encourage and motivate them. When giving feedback, you should make sure that it is always constructive, specific and developmental. It's important to keep your learners motivated, and what you say can help or hinder this.

Example

Raj had been progressing well throughout the programme. However, when the teacher marked his most recent assignment, he noticed that Raj had not met all the assessment criteria. Not wanting to demotivate Raj, the teacher wrote, 'Raj, you have made a really good attempt at addressing all the points of the assignment. However, criteria 1.3 just needs a little more to fully satisfy the requirements'. This feedback is much more encouraging than, 'You haven't met all the criteria, do it again'. Using the word 'however' is much better than using 'but', as 'but' is often perceived as negative.

Feedback can be written or verbal. If you are writing feedback to be read by learners at a later date, take into account that how you write it may not be how they read it. It's easy to interpret words or phrases differently from how they were intended, so, if you can, read the feedback to your learners at the time of returning their work. If you don't see your learners regularly, you could be marking their work at home and e-mailing feedback to them. If so, don't get too personal with this, keep to the facts but be as positive as possible to retain learner motivation. If you are giving individual verbal feedback, consider when and where you will do this, so as not to embarrass your learner in any way. Also, consider your tone of voice and take into account your learner's non-verbal signals when receiving feedback, to enable you to keep them motivated. You might give verbal feedback to a group regarding an activity; if so, make sure your feedback is specific to the group, and/or the individuals' contributions. Learners like to know how they are progressing, and what they need to do to improve or develop further. Simple statements such as 'well done' or 'good' don't tell the learner what was good about their work or how they can improve it. Using the learner's name makes the feedback more personal and making the feedback specific enables the learner to see what they need to do to improve.

Activity

Imagine you are giving individual feedback to Melvin, who has delivered a presentation to the group which should have lasted 10 minutes but took only five. The feedback will be given in front of his peers. What would you say?

You could begin with, 'Melvin, you have made a good attempt at your presentation. However, you didn't quite achieve your target of 10 minutes. You will have the opportunity to do this again next week, so I would recommend you plan extra material in advance to enable you to fully utilise the allotted time'. This feedback is specific and developmental to Melvin, who is made aware that he did not meet the requirements, but knows how to put this right next time. If you had said, 'Sorry, Melvin, but you've failed the activity', he would have felt very demotivated and might not wish to continue; he would also be embarrassed in front of his peers.

Peer feedback is useful for developing and motivating learners, and should be managed well. You need to give advice to your learners as to how to do this effectively without upsetting their peers. Sometimes, learners consider more what their peers are saying than what you might have to say.

You may need to keep records of feedback you give to your learners. For example, if you have carried out an observation, you should give a copy to your learner when giving feedback, and keep the original for your records. If you give written feedback to a learner about their assignment which requires further development, and this is written on their work, what record do you have of what you expected them to do if they lose this? You will need to check with your organisation what records they require you to keep.

Quality assurance

To ensure that you are teaching your subject correctly and effectively, and that learning is taking place, there are various activities your own organisation and external bodies will carry out. These may include:

- validating programmes for delivery;

- observations of teaching and learning;

- surveys and questionnaires;

- team meetings;

- standardising the practice of teaching and assessment;

- programme reviews and evaluations, including an analysis of retention and achievement;

- internal and external verification and moderation;

- following up, and analysing the reasons for complaints and appeals;

- reviewing policies and procedures;

- self assessment reports;

- external inspections and audits by funding bodies and inspectors.

Activity

Consider which of the above bullet points are most pertinent to your role as a teacher. Find out what quality assurance activities are in place at your organisation and whether you are due to be inspected at any time.

Your role as a teacher involves far more than just educating your learners; it's a long-term commitment which, hopefully, you will enjoy and find very rewarding.

This chapter contributes towards the following minimum core elements (see Appendix 2 for cross-references):

L2, L3, LS3, LL1, LR2, LW3;
PLR1, PLR2, PLR3, PLS1, PLS2, PLS3, PLS4;
NP2, NP3;
PNC3, PNC5, PNP3, PNP4, PNP5, PNP6; PNP7, PNP8;
ICT2;
ICTPC5;
ICT1, ICT5, ICTC1, ICTP1, ICTPC2, ICTPC3, ICTPP1, ICTPP2, ICTPP3

Summary

In this chapter you have learnt about:

- teaching and learning;

- integrating literacy, language, numeracy and ICT skills within the teaching context;

- assessment;

- feedback;

- quality assurance.

References and further information

Gravells A (2008) *Preparing to Teach in the Lifelong Learning Sector* (3rd edn), Exeter: Learning Matters.

Knowles M et al (2005) *The adult learner: the definitive classic in adult education and human resource development*, Oxford: Butterworth-Heinemann/Elsevier.

Laird D (1985) *Approaches to Training and Development*, Harlow: Addison Wesley.

Reece I Walker S (2007) *Teaching, Training and Learning* (6th edn), Sunderland: Business Education Publishers Ltd.

Tummons J (2008) *Assessing Learning in the Lifelong Learning Sector* (2nd edn), Exeter: Learning Matters.

Wallace S (2007) *Managing Behaviour in the Lifelong Learning Sector* (2nd edn), Exeter: Learning Matters.

Wallace S (2007) *Teaching, Training and Tutoring in the Lifelong Learning Sector* (3rd edn), Exeter: Learning Matters.

Websites

Cognitive Learning Styles – http://tip.psychology.org/styles.html

Dewey – http://www.infed.org/thinkers/et-dewey.htm

Functional Skills – http://www.qca.org.uk/qca_6062.aspx

Honey & Mumford Learning Styles – www.peterhoney.com

Neil Fleming Learning Styles – www.vark-learn.com

Oxford Brookes University Teaching & Learning – www.brookes.ac.uk

Theories of learning – www.learningandteaching.info/learning/

4 RESOURCES

Introduction

In this chapter you will learn about:

- resources and their use in a teaching and learning environment;
- new and emerging technologies;
- selecting, adapting and using resources;
- justifying the use of inclusive resources.

There are activities and examples to help you reflect on the above, which will assist your understanding of how to select, adapt, use and justify a range of inclusive resources which contribute to effective learning.

Guidance to address the minimum core of literacy, language, numeracy and information and communication technology (ICT) is integrated throughout and referenced at the end of the chapter.

Chapter 7 contains useful pro formas you may wish to use.

This chapter contributes towards the following: *scope* (S), *knowledge* (K) and *practice* (P) aspects of the professional standards (A–F domains) for teachers, tutors and trainers in the Lifelong Learning Sector:

AS1, AS2, AS3, AS4, AS5, AS6, AS7, AK3, AK4.1, AK4.2, AK4.3, AK5.1, AK6.1, AK7.1, AK7.2, AK7.3, AP3.1, AP4.1, AP4.2, AP4.3, AP5.1, AP5.2, AP6.1, AP6.2, AP7.2, AP7.3;
BS1, BS2, BS3, BS4, BS5, BK1.1, BK1.3, BK2.1, BK2.2, BK2.3, BK2.4, BK2.6, BK2.7, BP2.1, BP2.2, BP2.3, BP2.6, BP2.7, BP3.3, BP5.1, BP5.2;
CS1, CS2, CS3, CS4, CK2.1, CK3.3, CK3.4, CK3.5, CP2.1, CP3.2, CP3.3, CP3.4, CP3.5;
DS1, DS2, DS3, DK1.1, DK1.3, DK2.1, DK2.2, DK3.1, DK3.2, DP1.1, DP1.3, DP2.1, DP2.2, DP3.1, DP3.2.

The standards can be accessed at:
http://www.lluk.org.uk/documents/ professional_standards_for_itts_020107.pdf

Resources and their use in a teaching and learning environment

Resources are a valuable aid when teaching and will help you reach the differing learning styles, needs and potential of your learners. They include the use of equipment, handouts, presentations, people, books and the internet etc. All resources you use should meet the different needs of your learners, promote equality, support diversity and contribute to effective learning.

A resource is described as something which can be turned to for support or help, or an available supply of something to be drawn upon when needed (Grolier 1981). Resources are media which should be used effectively and to their best advantage.

When you take responsibility for planning, designing and teaching a learning programme, you must consider which resources you will need. These resources should aid teaching and learning to enable the learning outcomes to be achieved. You will want your learners to enjoy their programme and find the learning experience interesting. It's important that the resources you use are varied and take account of the different needs and styles of your learners. You will find there is a wealth of resources already available; for example, via specialist websites, publishing companies, Awarding/Examining bodies and external agencies, and many of these are available free. It may be your responsibility to research, select, adapt and use a variety of materials to effectively support the learning process. A resource should be relevant to learning, clearly laid out or described, well presented, up to date, adaptable and purposeful.

Resources come in many different guises and you need to find out what resources are available to you in your organisation and how you can access them. Designing and creating resources can take up a lot of time, so find out first of all what is already available; often it's easier and quicker to adapt a resource than to create a new one. Ask experienced colleagues and your programme manager which resources they use in their teaching and what they recommend. Ask them also if you can go along and observe the way in which they use a particular resource, to get ideas. Make contact with the support staff in your organisation; for example, to help word process or photocopy work for you.

The following list gives some examples of the *physical* resources you may find available in most organisations:

- accommodation and appropriate furniture;
- audio equipment (plus speakers, headphones);
- computers, laptops and other ICT-related equipment;
- equipment (binding machine, laminator, photocopier);

- handouts/worksheets;

- internet connectivity (laptops with wireless internet access);

- programme information (syllabus, Awarding/Examination body materials, assessment documents);

- specialist equipment to support learners;

- stationery;

- televisions/DVDs/CD-ROMs/videos;

- whiteboards (including interactive), boards and flipcharts.

A more comprehensive list can be found in Appendix 4.

Accommodation and furniture will vary from building to building. Well-established learning organisations will be suitably furnished, and the person responsible for allocating accommodation to programmes will be required to take into account the needs of the learners. The Learning and Skills Council (LSC) allocates funding to training organisations. This is to ensure that their buildings are comfortable and safe for adult learners, and meet the requirements of the Disability Discrimination Act 1995 (extended to include education from 2002). However, you may be asked to teach in outreach accommodation where standards will vary from place to place. Your organisation should have agreed minimum standards which all learning environments are required to meet or adhere to. Learners should be informed of the facilities available at your organisation, either before enrolling, or at the commencement of their programme.

Whiteboards (including interactive whiteboards) are very effective when used to demonstrate topics. Demonstrations can be interactive and learners can participate in activities such as online quizzes. When using the whiteboard, be careful that the focus is on the learner and not on the teacher. If sessions are too long the learners will not maintain their interest and will lose their motivation. Do consider learners with disabilities or learning difficulties – for example, visually impaired or dyslexic learners – and ensure that all learning needs are being met. The best way of finding out if you are meeting learners' needs is to ask them.

During a session, you should always have stationery, pens, board markers and the basic equipment necessary to ensure its smooth running. This shows your learners you are well organised; for example, if you have different coloured flipchart pens to hand, you don't need to leave the room to locate them. These items may be costly and may not always be available. If you are working in outreach centres you may have to transport heavy resources, which can be difficult and time-consuming. Advance booking may also be required for some equipment and resources.

Electronic equipment in all its guises, i.e. computers, DVDs, televisions, audio equipment etc, can be used as tools for engaging with learners and offering choice to the learners about the way in which they learn. Many subject areas now use computers, digital cameras, mobile phones etc to enhance learning and captivate the learners' interest. Such equipment also encourages the learners to be more independent in their learning, in that they can access information and materials in their own time. Activities during the session can also be varied according to learning styles; for example, one learner may prefer to read a script and another may prefer to watch and listen to a video clip of the same subject via a website. However, not all venues have internet-connected computers, sometimes the equipment is old and out of date, there may be variations in software available, and sometimes it just won't work. Information found via the internet is not always accurate; therefore, learners need to be warned about this. Again, you may need to book any specialised equipment in advance.

The resources you require will depend on the learning environment and will link to the different methods of teaching you have planned. If you are teaching in the workplace or in a workshop, using genuine objects and materials from the vocational setting can make the learning more relevant and meaningful. This addresses the concept of purposeful learning: *purposeful* activities enable learners to use a wide range of skills to work in a team and to gain real experiences and support. When teaching a skill, a handout or worksheet may not be as useful as the *real thing*.

Example

Jonathan, a playgroup manager, is teaching the Level 3 Diploma in Playwork to a group of learners who are all employed in this field, i.e. they all work in after-school clubs or childcare settings. He has decided to demonstrate the use of puppets as a valuable resource in communicating with a young child. This is an extremely relevant resource, enhanced by Jonathan's own experiences in this field. The learners are being taught using a resource that they will also be able to use in their practice.

Resources which can be related to the occupational setting and can be contextualised will support the learner in applying the knowledge and understanding outside of their learning environment. These are known as *transferable skills*. It may be more of a challenge to select, adapt and use a range of resources in a work-related context; however, differentiating learning in this way is critical to meeting the needs of the learners.

Activity

Think about a worksheet or handout you have used with your learners. Consider whether you chose the most appropriate format for this resource. Could it have been used in a more active and purposeful way – how would you change or adapt it?

You might have thought about using larger text, including some graphics, using colour or rephrasing your words or questions. You also need to ensure that all text is legible and at the correct level for the learner. Always evaluate how effective your resources are, to enable you to improve them for the future.

When designing or using a resource, you need to consider how adaptable it can be to be used in other formats. One size does not fit all, therefore resources may need to be adapted to suit particular learner needs. Everyone is different, but all your learners deserve to be treated with an equal level of respect and have equal access to the programme resources. Be proactive in coping with differences by talking to your learners and finding out exactly what they require so that their learning is effective from the start of their programme. When you are considering any required changes or alterations to resources, you must make sure they are reasonable. You should keep in mind that your organisation has a legal responsibility under the Disability Discrimination Act (1995, amended 2005) to anticipate the likely needs of disabled learners. Provision for disabled learners should be made in advance, i.e. your organisation should not just respond to the individual needs of one learner to the detriment of others. However, situations will always arise that are not accounted for, and this is when your skills as a teacher should come to the fore.

Example

Kathryn has difficulty reading black text printed on a white background. During enrolment she did disclose that she had a disability and required additional support. The teacher did not see the enrolment form prior to the first class and was therefore not aware of this. Kathryn did make the teacher aware at the end of the session that she had difficulty with the colour of the computerised presentation and the handouts. Her learning during this session was therefore ineffective. The teacher addressed this for future sessions and printed Kathryn's resources on a green background to enable her learning to be effective.

You should find out as much as you possibly can about your learners prior to your first meeting with them. Learners will often decide at the first session whether or not they will return to the next session. First impressions are very important to ensure that your learner has a positive experience and remains with you throughout the programme.

Health and safety with regard to the use of equipment and training materials is imperative, and there are procedures required by the Health and Safety at Work Act (1974) which must be followed. It may be that you are using resources which have not previously been used; you may therefore need training, or be required to carry out a risk assessment to ensure their safe use.

You should be aware that your learners also have a personal responsibility to be mindful of their own and other people's safety, and you have a duty of care towards them.

Example

John is teaching a Do-It-Yourself programme to a mixed group of adults in an Adult Community Learning Centre. He has been teaching this group for a number of years and knows most of them really well. In this class the learners are using battery-powered drills to make holes in pieces of wood. They have used these drills before and John therefore assumed they knew the procedures regarding health and safety and did not cover them during this session. One particularly important health and safety point is that only one learner touches and uses the drill at any one time. One drill was not working properly and John was busy elsewhere; a learner held the drill bit while another learner tried to switch it on. John saw what was happening and yelled across the room. A serious accident was averted – this time.

The following list gives some examples of the human resources you could utilise within your organisation:

- teachers;
- colleagues;
- visiting speakers;
- expert witnesses;
- mentors;
- Awarding/Examining body personnel;
- support staff;
- technicians.

Teachers are one of the most effective resources available to learners. Learners who can identify with a good learning experience usually state that this is first and foremost because of the teacher. Having a passion for your subject is infectious, as you use your skills and knowledge to enhance your learners. You may not know everything, but be honest with your learners about this and assure them that you will find out the answers. Visiting speakers may bring a different new approach with their expertise but do ensure that they are *experts* in their field – only use speakers you have prior experience of or who are recommended from a trusted source. Colleagues and mentors are a vital source of expertise in developing both your knowledge and your teaching skills in your specialist area. Ensure that you establish relationships with colleagues from across the organisation and also in partner organisations to benefit from the exchange of expertise. Expert witnesses and mentors in, for example, the workplace provide a vital source of support for your learners. It is important that your learners feel comfortable with these people and that the mentors have the time to commit to this aspect of learning. They need to have some knowledge of the programme and be able to apply it to a work-based context. Support workers can give help to learners who declare a disability or learning difficulty and are a lifeline to learning, both for the teacher and the learner. It's important that they are informed and directed about the individual's learning programme. They should be wary of the learner becoming too dependent or reliant upon their support. It's your responsibility to develop independence in your learners and you need to be particularly aware of this.

New and emerging technologies

Information and learning technology (ILT) refers to the use of information and communication technologies to support the core business of your organisation, i.e. the delivery and management of learning. ILT is an umbrella term for the entire computer industry and covers a wide range of technologies which are developing and changing constantly. Within the content of your learning programme you will need to identify opportunities that this valuable resource provides to develop your learners' skills and knowledge. E-learning includes the use of electronic learning technologies; for example data projectors, interactive whiteboards, virtual learning environments (VLEs) and the teaching and learning methods that they encompass. If someone is learning in a way that uses any information and communication technologies – for example, computers and other equipment and software – they are using e-learning.

Learners learn in many different ways and at different times. To support these different learning needs, there are different e-learning teaching methods. Classroom technology use might involve all your learners sitting in front of networked computers while you guide their learning using a data projector from a computer. Many learners may prefer or need to learn when and where it is convenient for them. This may mean distance learning either from home or elsewhere; for example, in another part of the country. Synchronous learning enables learning to take place via a virtual classroom and duplicates the capabilities found in a real classroom. The teacher and learners log on at set times. This provides:

- a place to meet: teachers and learners use their computers to go to a virtual meeting place instead of a classroom;
- an attendance register: a record is made of learners logging on;
- facilitation of learning: teachers can choose from a variety of synchronous technologies including:
  - slide presentation,
  - audio and video conferencing,
  - application sharing,
  - shared whiteboard;
- interaction with learners: learners can indicate when they want to speak by virtually raising their hand. Teachers can enable learners to speak through audio and video conferencing. Teachers and learners can use instant messaging and chat rooms;
- quizzes: teachers can present questions to learners;

- breakout sessions: learners can work together in groups;

- assessment: feedback and records are maintained.

Most companies that sell virtual classroom software provide all of these capabilities in a single package.

Asynchronous learning is learning that happens anywhere and at any time. Learners are able to interact with resource materials, and with their teachers and each other at a time of their choosing. Learners across different time zones and different continents can participate in the same programmes. Content can be explored and discussed in great depth – allowing learners the time to reflect and formulate thoughtful responses. A discussion thread is an example of asynchronous learning. One learner can post a question, and hours (or days) later, another learner can post a response. Asynchronous tools like e-mail and discussion forums have trans-formed the way learners communicate and share knowledge.

Asynchronous learning gives e-learning much of its appeal. Traditionally, learners needed to be physically present to engage with teachers and other learners. Now, learners can engage with each other when it is most convenient, and a *knowledge thread* or trail of their postings is left. Teachers should be specifically trained to teach using this style and method of teaching.

You need to establish exactly what technology is available in your organisation and how this is supported at the time and place you are teaching. You may be teaching in a college environment and therefore have access to all their technology and technical support. Do you know if they would be available at 8.30 p.m. on a Thursday when you are teaching? You may, however, be teaching in a community building with restrictions to the systems and no internet connection. You will need to take account of this when deciding which resources you will use in your teach-ing and to make sure that they work.

Never make assumptions about technology. Always check the equipment personally and in the context in which you are planning to use it. Always have a contingency plan in case of technical failure at the time you are teaching. If it's at all possible, request that assistance from technical support staff be on hand if you are using a piece of technology for the first time. There may be staff called *E-Guide co-ordinators* or *ILT Champions* whose job it is to help teachers integrate ILT into their specialist subject area. You need to find out who these people are and ask for a training ses-sion if you're not fully confident using the equipment or programmes. They should be able to demonstrate examples of e-learning in your specialist area. You can then identify clear benefits to your learners; for example, learning from home using materials stored on the organisation's *learning platform*.

ILT covers a much wider range of technologies than just computers. Some of these are:

- computer hardware and software; for example, to produce a presentation, using an interactive board to write notes, enabling these to be saved, printed or e-mailed;

- digital cameras, camcorders, scanners and other image-capturing equipment; for example, to take digital photographs of completed work;

- interactive whiteboards; for example, to view demonstrations;

- digital television, video, audio and other related multimedia equipment; for example, to watch and listen to video clips;

- mobile phones; for example, to contact your learners, take photos and video clips;

- learning platforms; for example, an area provided by your organisation via the internet which learners can access to find electronic resources relevant to their programme;

- calculators, graphic calculators;

- personal digital assistants, voting technology;

- video-conferencing, using web cameras; for example, linking up with a session being delivered elsewhere, perhaps by a visiting speaker in another organisation.

Whichever media you decide to use, ensure that it is being used for a meaningful purpose. Purposeful use of ICT provides your learners with a reason to use and engage with the technology – a real-life activity that ensures your learners understand why they are using the technology and what benefits they are getting from it.

Example

Naila is teaching and assessing the Level 2 NVQ in Youth Work programme. She has two learners who, due to work commitments, are unable to attend the weekly knowledge sessions she delivers on a Monday evening. Naila makes use of the organisation's learning platform and uploads the session plan and any handouts or worksheets for these learners so that they can access them from home.

During induction, you need to inform your learners what the programme expectations are in terms of ILT. It is important that your learners know to what extent they will be expected to access and use ILT, and how to go about this, either at the organisation or elsewhere. You may wish to communicate with your learners via e-mail, and expect them to access materials on a learning platform or via an intranet (an organisation's private computer network). Your organisation may also have networked computers and your learners may benefit from storing their own work and resources in an allocated network area. It is particularly important that all learners are clear about how they achieve this and what to do if they are experiencing any difficulties. Learners should always be encouraged to make back-up copies of any work.

Your learners will also need to be made aware of your organisation's policy regarding the use of computers and the internet, to which they must comply.

It is important to establish with your learners during initial assessment whether or not they have existing skills and knowledge and to what extent. For those learners who may have difficulty using and accessing ICT, you need to ensure that they have access to the support they require.

The following are some possible activities which could be integrated into your teaching:

- using a blog: this is a portmanteau (fusion of two words) of *web* and *log* and is a website where entries are commonly displayed in reverse chronological order; for example, a learning diary;

- taking photographs or videos, downloading them onto a computer and either printing, viewing during a session or posting to a website;

- creating a webpage;

- using e-mail to communicate with your learners and to encourage learners to e-mail each other between sessions;

- using online discussion forums;

- accessing electronic templates and forms from a virtual learning environment (VLE) and using interactive activities.

In March 2005, the Department for Education and Skills published the e-Strategy *Harnessing Technology: Transforming learning and children's services.* The Department believes that teachers need a more strategic approach to the future development of ICT in education, skills and children's services.

A greater focus on technology will produce real benefits for all. Parents and carers could see more about what their children are learning in school or college through their website. Employers and communities could access ICT training and support more readily. Young people and adult learners should be able to see programmes tailored to their personal needs, and progress more easily through different organisations at different stages of their lives. And those working in education and children's services will benefit from more online support and technological solutions to problems of assessment and administration.

Selecting, adapting and using resources

Too often teaching is worksheet- and handout-driven. Using resources and materials effectively in order to support learning is challenging and exciting for you as a teacher, and engages and motivates your learners. Be creative and innovative when selecting and/or developing resources for your programme.

> *What the learner does is more important than what the teacher does.*
> www.geoffpetty.com

Geoff Petty's theory of active learning states that we *learn by doing.* Active learning is much better recalled, enjoyed and understood, and requires your learners to *make their own meaning* of their learning. When you consider what the criteria are for selecting your resources, remember that these resources should help the learner use their learning in realistic and useful ways. A good teacher will select and use resources which centre around the learner, and they tend to be more fun, ensuring that learning is interesting and memorable.

Selecting, developing and/or adapting learning materials requires an in-depth knowledge of the programme and subject you are teaching. The qualification will contain certain objectives/learning outcomes which your learners will be required to achieve if they are to be successful. If you are teaching a programme which doesn't have a qualification, there will be a curriculum to follow with a syllabus. This may be produced by your organisation, or you may have to produce it yourself. The resources you use in your teaching will need to relate to the qualification and/or curriculum requirements.

Wherever possible, resources should reflect the learners' interests. These may include a range of occupational, vocational, community, cultural and/or family interests.

Example

Maureen teaches Level One ICT to football apprentices at the local football club as part of their wider NVQ Sports Science qualification. Her learners live and breathe football. During the first year of teaching Maureen used the standard worksheet resources available in the organisation and experienced a lack of motivation and a lot of disruption from uninterested learners. In preparation for the next group, Maureen redesigned the worksheets so that they were all football related, although still meeting the learning outcomes of the curriculum. She also researched the availability of embedding learning materials in literacy, numeracy and ICT and used the 'Heading for Success' DfES project (Heading for Success, DfES 2006). These materials provide a combined approach to football and ICT. Although only a third of the way through their programme, the apprentices have already achieved two of the three units required towards the full qualification. Poor retention and achievement were overcome.

Enabling learners to choose projects that reflect their own interests will help motivation.

Activity

Make a list of resources you have either developed or used in the past. What was the focus of each? Was it relevant? Could the resources be adapted for learners with different interests or needs?

It's possible you may have updated or revised many of your resources, either based on feedback, the success (or otherwise) of their use or to meet any particular learner needs. It's advisable to talk to other teachers in your subject area, to see if you can swap or adapt resources for use with your learners.

Learners in post-16 education are very diverse; you may, for example, have a learner whose first language is not English and who therefore needs more time to understand the generic language, before learning the subject or topic. Therefore, using a wide variety of resources will engage and motivate your learners, meeting the range of needs. There are many differences between learners that affect their learning. Differentiation is about coping with these differences and using them to promote learning. Differentiated learning needs to take into account that your learners may differ in terms of:

- their motivation;
- prior experience and knowledge;
- learning support needs;
- cultural expectations;
- literacy, language, numeracy and ICT levels;
- learning preferences.

When developing and/or using resources, consider that there may be a need for:

- more than one level of difficulty
  - produce exercises which meet the core learning outcomes, with additional, more complex activities for stronger learners; for example, *build-up* and extension exercises which help extend the scope of capable learners;
- the use of different media, including ICT and interactive resources
  - integrate this in your sessions, keeping the format and content varied and interesting;
- additional learning support for individuals or small groups
  - arrange for a learning support worker (if possible) to work with learners who declare they have a learning disability or difficulty;
  - refer to a literacy, language or ICT specialist if it is appropriate.

It may be that you feel you require some training in developing and using resources. There may be continuing professional development (CPD) opportunities for you to access within your team, your organisation or via national bodies like NIACE (National Institute of Adult Continuing Education).

Example

Lindsay was a teacher of English for Speakers of Other Languages (ESOL) for many years and then took a career break. On returning to teaching she has discovered interactive whiteboards and computers in all the classrooms. She would like her learners to access relevant websites during the sessions but doesn't have the confidence to use the equipment. Lindsay does use a word processor for preparing her planning documents, worksheets and handouts. Lindsay contacts her programme leader for support and assistance with embedding ICT into her sessions.

It might be useful to find out if there is an E-Guide or ICT support worker in your organisation, and if they could support a couple of your sessions to help build your confidence in using the ICT equipment. It might not be as daunting as it first seems.

Justifying the use of inclusive resources

When you are about to teach a programme for the first time you should ask about the accessibility of equipment and resources for you to use. You may find that there isn't an abundance of resources available and you may have to develop your own. In some cases there might be some resources available but perhaps not what you would normally choose to use. You may decide to use or adapt these, particularly if you are asked to teach a programme at short notice. Some teachers do not like using resources created by other teachers and prefer to create their own. In most subject areas there are published resources available to purchase but some of these can be expensive. You should feel able to ask at your organisation if resources can be purchased; however, it may not always be possible for financial reasons. If you do make such a request you may have to present a feasibility study relating to the programme needs and requirements. It is possible that you could find lots of free resources by carrying out a search via the internet for your particular subject.

If you need to use reprographic equipment, always err on the side of caution; check that the equipment is working, and allow time for photocopying. It may be that you have to send your materials to a central location to be copied and this will take longer than if a photocopier is available for you to use yourself. You might be allocated a budget for copying and when this has run out you can't do any more. If your learners have access to e-mail or your organisation's learning platform, you could encourage them to access or print the necessary resources they need.

There may be other resources and help available in your organisation; for example, support for the production of word-processed handouts, use of library facilities for borrowing books and accessing other useful resources such as journals, DVDs, newspapers etc. Perhaps you can book a session for your learners at the library or resource centre, with a member of staff who can explain and demonstrate how the system works. Not all organisations have library or resource facilities and you may have to find out from your local public library what books, ICT facilities and other useful resources they may have for learners to borrow or use.

You should check any copyright and data protection regulations for any materials you decide to use. The Copyright Act 1998 covers copying, adapting and distributing materials, including computer programmes and materials found via the internet. It may be that you will have to ask the author's permission to use their materials and they may need to be acknowledged for their work on your resource.

Using the *who, what, when, where, why* and *how* rationale is a good basis for determining how relevant, purposeful and effective your resource will be.

Always have a clear rationale to justify the resources you have chosen and evaluate them afterwards to help you improve your session for the next time.

This chapter contributes towards the following minimum core elements (see Appendix 2 for cross-references)

L2, L3, L5, L6, L8, LS2, LS3, LL1, LR1, LR2, LR3, LW1, LW3;
PLL1, PLR1, PLR2, PLR3, PLW1, PLW2, PLW3, PLW4;
ICT1, ICT2, ICT3, ICT5, ICTP1, ICTP2, ICTP3, ICTPC1, ICTPC2, ICTPC3, ICTPC4, ICTPC5, ICTPP1, ICTPP2, ICTPP3.

Summary

In this chapter you have learnt about:

- resources and their use in a teaching and learning environment;

- new and emerging technologies;

- selecting, adapting and using resources;

- justifying the use of inclusive resources.

References and further information

Daines J W et al (2006) *Adult Learning, Adult Teaching* (4th edn) Cardiff: Welsh Academic Press.

DfES (2003) *Success in adult literacy, numeracy and ESOL provision: a guide to support the CIF.*

DfES (2004) *Planning Learning, Recording Progress and Reporting Achievement – a guide for practitioners.*

DfES (2005) *Harnessing Technology: Transforming Learning and Children's Services.*

DfES (2006) *Heading for Success.*

Grolier (1981) *New Book of Knowledge Dictionary, Volume 1*, Boston MA: Houghton Mifflin Co.

Hill C (2008) *Teaching with e-learning in the Lifelong Learning Sector*, Exeter: Learning Matters.

Knowles M S et al (2005) *The adult learner: the definitive classic in adult education and human resource development*, Oxford: Butterworth-Heinemann/Elsevier.

Mager R F (1984) *Preparing instructional objectives* (2nd edn), Belmont CA: David S Lake.

Minton D (2005) *Teaching Skills in Further and Adult Education* (3rd edn), Florence, KY: Thomson Learning.

Skills for Business (June 2007) Literacy, Language, Numeracy and ICT *Adults Learning* (December 2, Volume 19, Number 4).

Websites

Copyright Act – http://www.opsi.gov.uk/acts/acts1988/Ukpga_19880048_en_1.htm

Data Protection Act – http://www.opsi.gov.uk/acts/acts1998/ukpga_19980029_en_1

Exploring informal education, lifelong learning and social action – www.infed.co.uk

Geoff Petty – www.geoffpetty.com

Heading for Success, 2006 – http://www.dfes.gov.uk/readwriteplus/Heading_for_Success

Health and Safety at Work Act 1974 – http://www.hse.gov.uk/legislation/hswa.htm

Learning and Skills Network – www.lsneducation.org.uk

National Research and Development Centre – www.nrdc.org.uk

National Institute of Adult Continuing Education – www.niace.org.uk

Quality Improvement Agency – www.excellence.qia.org.uk

Introduction

In this chapter you will learn about:

- communication skills;

- verbal and non-verbal communication;

- working with individuals, and small and large groups;

- managing behaviour and disruption;

- motivation.

There are activities and examples to help you reflect on the above, which will assist your understanding of how to communicate effectively.

Guidance to address the minimum core of literacy, language, numeracy and information and communication technology (ICT) is integrated throughout and referenced at the end of the chapter.

Chapter 7 contains useful pro formas you may wish to use.

This chapter contributes towards the following: *scope* (S), *knowledge* (K) and *practice* (P) aspects of the professional standards (A–F domains) for teachers, tutors and trainers in the Lifelong Learning Sector.

AS1, AS2, AS5, AK1.1, AK2.1, AK2.2, AK3.1, AK4.1, AK4.2, AK5.1, AK5.2, AP1.1, AP2.1, AP4.1, AP5.1, AP5.2;
BS1, BS2, BS3, BS4, BK1.2, BK2.1, BK2.2, BK3.1, BK3.2, BK3.4 BK3.5, BK4.1, BP1.1, BP1.2, BP2.2, BP2.4, BP2.5, BP3.1, BP3.2, BP3.3, BP3.4, BP3.5, BP4.1;
CS4, CK2.1, CK3.1, CK3.2, CK3.3, CK3.4, CK4.2, CP2.1, CP3.1, CP3.2, CP4.2.

The standards can be accessed at: http://www.lluk.org.uk/documents/professional_standards_for_itts_020107.pdf

Communication skills

Communication is a means of passing on information from one person to another; it can be verbal, non-verbal or written.

One of the skills of communicating effectively is projecting *confidence*. You may not feel confident when meeting a new group for the first time; you may feel quite nervous. Imagine though that you are an actor playing a role, and try to keep relaxed, calm, composed and focused. Your knowledge of, and passion for, your subject will help your confidence. You also need to be organised and plan what you want to communicate and how you are going to do this. Your learners don't know what you know, that's why they want to learn. So keep things simple and don't try to achieve too much; it takes time to assimilate new skills and knowledge.

Empathy and *sympathy* are also skills of communication. You can express empathy when you have personally experienced something your learner has gone through. You can only sympathise when you haven't. However, don't be too keen to reveal to your learners personal information about yourself. You may feel you are gaining their confidence but you might also lose their respect. Don't get too friendly with your learners, keep the relationship professional at all times. Learners may tell you things that need to remain confidential, or they may discuss things with you that you cannot deal with, therefore you may need to liaise with others if necessary.

You may have barriers which prevent you from communicating effectively. For example, you might plan to introduce a complex topic to your learners, which could be misinterpreted if not conveyed in a logical order. Poor body language, voice projection and/or handouts with too much text or containing spelling errors will lead to confusion. Speaking too quickly or giving too much factual information too fast will not allow learners time to assimilate their new knowledge. Your learners may also have barriers; they may have preoccupations which lead to lapses in concentration, or they may not understand the terminology you are using. They may have had previous educational experiences which were not good, or have cultural differences which may have an impact upon their literacy and language learning. Initial assessment may help with your understanding of their needs. Once you are aware of any issues – yours or your learners' – you can work on them and communicate in a way that enables your learners to interpret what you are conveying, in the way you intended.

You may also need to communicate with others at work; for example, colleagues, managers, Awarding/Examining body verifiers, funding inspectors etc. The way you do this will also help to form others' impressions of yourself. You may have to attend meetings or video conferences, and wherever you are with other people, they will make assumptions about you based upon what they see and hear. You may have to write reports or memos, and the way you express yourself when writing is as important as when you are speaking. Always remain professional; leave any personal issues behind, otherwise these will impact upon your teaching and your job role.

However, your main communication will be with your learners, so you need to ensure that what you are communicating is accurate, not ambiguous or biased and is expressed in a professional manner. Show your professionalism, not only in what you say, but in the way you say it, and in your attitude, your body language and your dress. A warm and confident smile, a positive attitude, self-assurance and the use of eye contact will put both you and your learners at ease. Remember, you never get a second chance to make a first impression.

Activity

Ask a colleague or your mentor to observe one of your teaching sessions. They could use the pro forma in Chapter 7. Their feedback will be valuable towards your development. Alternatively, make a visual recording of your own teaching, and watch this afterwards. You may be surprised at what you see; perhaps mannerisms you weren't aware of when communicating, such as waving your hands about or repeatedly saying 'um'.

Listening is an important communication skill. You may be able to convey your message to your learners effectively, but if you can't listen to what they say, or answer their questions satisfactorily, communication will break down; it should be a two-way process. Alternatively, you may be distracted by external noises and may not be able to concentrate on what is being said at the time. If a learner asks a question, repeat it to enable the full group to hear it, and to show that you have heard it correctly. Hearing what is said is different from listening to what is going on in the room. You may need to pay more attention and to keep focused on what your learners are saying. Active listening involves listening with a purpose; that is, to hear what you want to hear and still remain able to listen to all that is being said without letting other things distract you. If you find it hard to remember what is being said, repeat key words or make notes to help you. This is a skill you can encourage your learners to use.

Activity

Listen to the news on the radio (aural) and then again on the television (visual and aural). Do you hear things differently if you can only hear them, rather than seeing as well? Do you make any assumptions about the person who is speaking? Do you really hear everything that is being said, or do you listen only to the parts that interest you? Are you distracted by other things happening at the time?

What someone says and what you hear can be very different. Often, our personal assumptions and beliefs can distort what we hear. Try to use active listening, repeating back or summarising what was said, to ensure that you have understood. If you are unsure what someone has said, ask them to repeat it or say, 'Have I understood you correctly? Did you mean....?' Feedback is a verbal communication skill that clearly demonstrates that you are actively listening, and confirms the communication between you and your learners.

Understanding a little about your own personal communication style will help you create a lasting impression upon your learners and enable you to become a better listener. If you are aware of how others see and hear you, you can adapt to suit their style of learning.

The four skills of language are *speaking, listening, reading* and *writing*. Using these effectively will help to improve your ability to demonstrate the minimum core.

There are several theories regarding communication, group work and motivation; for example, Tuckman's (1965) Group Formation and Maslow's (1960) Hierarchy of Needs. Both of these are covered in the companion book *Preparing to Teach in the Lifelong Learning Sector* (Gravells 2008). A few others are covered briefly within this chapter, and you may wish to research these further.

Verbal and non-verbal communication

When communicating verbally, your tone, pace and inflections are all important factors in getting your message across. If you speak too quickly or softly, your learners may not hear everything you say. Always try and speak clearly, and a little more loudly and slowly than normal, particularly if you are talking to a group where learners are not in close proximity, or if you have a strong regional accent. The words you use should reflect equality and inclusiveness and should not be biased in any way. You may have learners for whom English is not their first language; therefore you will need to be careful with your use of words that they may not be familiar with, or even with your pronunciation. It's useful to consider what reactions you want to elicit from your learners to the information you are communicating. If your learners react differently, you will need to amend your methods. Watching your learners' body language will help you. However, you may be speaking one-to-one via the telephone, and so will be unable to see your learner's reactions to your words. This could lead to a misunderstanding. Always ask questions to check that the learner you are communicating with has understood things in the way you intended to convey. All communication should be appropriate to the learners, the subject and the level of study.

Example

A new learner has walked into your room by mistake. They soon realise and ask for directions to the correct room. As you are very familiar with the building, you give verbal directions. However, you can tell by the look on the learner's face that they are getting confused. You decide to draw a diagram, which gives clear directions, enabling the learner to visualise where they are going. Your communication is therefore appropriate to the learner.

The following checklist will help you when communicating verbally:

- speak clearly and a little more louder/slower than normal, emphasising new or unusual words. Be conscious of your accent, pitch and tone;

- be aware of your posture, gestures and body language, even if you are not in face-to-face contact, as these can help with your verbal expression;

- ensure that you have the required subject knowledge, introducing and conveying this confidently, convincingly, passionately and enthusiastically;

- introduce points in a logical order, avoiding ambiguity;

- back up explanations with handouts and/or visuals;

- emphasise key words and summarise key points regularly;

- allow time for questions (from you and your learners) but don't get too side-tracked by these;

- use learners' names;

- listen to your learners and watch for their reactions;

- recognise group dynamics, encourage shy learners and manage over-confident ones;

- use active listening skills;

- try not to say *um, yeah, okay, you know,* or *does that make sense?* (the latter may gain only a *yes* response, as learners feel that is what you want to hear; ask open questions instead);

- give constructive and positive feedback.

Non-verbal communication includes your body language and posture; for example, your gestures, and the way you stand or sit. Do be conscious of your mannerisms, such as folded arms, hands in pockets, characteristic gestures, and use eye contact with all your learners. Always pay attention to personal grooming, and dress appropriately for the subject you are teaching. For example, smart clothes are preferable if you are teaching business studies, but an overall is a necessity if you are teaching in a laboratory. Your learners will observe your dress, manner, attitude and language. This is often called the *hidden curriculum* (Jackson 1968). Your learners will subconsciously gain knowledge and attitudes from you. These may be aspects you do not actively teach but instead convey with your mannerisms and actions. Always make sure you are on time to sessions, preferably arriving early to ensure that the room is ready for use. If you don't have to rush to another session when you finish, stay around for a few minutes; you may find that learners will talk to you or ask questions they might not have felt they could during the session. The things you *don't* say are as important as those you *do* say.

The following checklist will help you with non-verbal communication:

- dress appropriately, act professionally and confidently;

- be aware of your posture, gestures and body language;

- use eye contact;

- position yourself so that all your learners can see you;

- don't fiddle with things;

- don't fold your arms or keep your hands in your pockets;

- observe your learners' reactions and their body language, and react to these.

Written communication – for example, in the form of feedback for assessed work, an e-mail, text message, handouts or a computerised presentation – is also an expression of yourself. Think carefully about how you phrase your words, to avoid misunderstandings; otherwise the meaning interpreted by your learners may not be the one you intended to convey. If you are working with learners via an online programme, you may never see them, but will probably build up a visual image; similarly, they may be doing the same of you. Information can easily be misinterpreted, so the sender has to be sure that the receiver will interpret any communication in the way that it was intended. You need to get your message across clearly and effectively, to avoid a breakdown in communication. Your writing style, words and syntax need to be checked for spelling, grammar and punctuation. Don't rely on a computer spellcheck or grammar checker, as this will not always pick up the context in which you are writing.

Technology is being used increasingly in education; learning can take place via a computer, with messages and questions posted and responded to, and teacher feedback given to learners. If you use this medium for communication and/or assessment purposes, try not to get in the habit of abbreviating words or cutting out vowels. It is important to express yourself in a professional way, to minimise the risk of misunderstanding and confusion. Imagine that you are talking to your learner face to face, and phrase your message appropriately.

The following checklist will help when communicating in writing:

- keep sentences short and to the point;
- don't include too many facts or dates;
- use visuals if possible;
- keep your text logical and progressive;
- use subject headings, underlining, bullets or bold type to emphasise points;
- avoid slang words, abbreviations, symbols or too much jargon;
- don't cut out vowels;
- proofread your work for spelling, grammar, punctuation, syntax;
- ensure pronouns are correctly spelled;
- check to see if anything could be misinterpreted;
- ensure your text covers equality, differentiation and inclusiveness;
- express numbers as words when the number is less than 10, or begins a sentence (e.g. 'Five days later' …). The number 10, or anything greater than 10, should be written as a figure (… 'there were 15 in the group.');
- don't raise any questions which are left unanswered;
- use Harvard referencing if you are including quotes from theorists.

When you are designing and using learning materials, for example, handouts or activities, ensure that they give positive images in terms of gender, disability, age, culture and ethnicity. Never assume that your message will be understood in the way you intended. Always clarify the content of any handouts you give to your learners and ask questions to check their understanding. When you ask your learners to carry out an activity, state clearly its purpose and expected outcome, encouraging your learners to ask questions to clarify any aspects of which they are unsure. Knowing your learners will help you adapt any learning materials accordingly. However, this may be difficult if you are teaching a one-off session and have no prior knowledge of your group. If the latter is the case, asking your learners to introduce themselves (or each other) as part of an icebreaker will help you discover a little about them. Failing to understand who you are communicating with may result in misunderstandings.

Activity

Think back to a training session or event you have recently attended. What do you remember about it? Do you remember the facilitator's mannerisms, the environment or the facilities? Or did you manage to focus on the topic you wanted to learn about?

The only reason the facilitator was there was to communicate information to you. However, you will have remembered other things, perhaps what the facilitator was wearing, how they spoke, the equipment they used, the refreshments you had or your experiences of networking with others. Look at this experience now from the perspective of your own learners; they too will remember a lot of other things besides the message you want to convey. To help them remain focused on your subject, keep your communications concise and clear, using examples to bring points to life; ask regular questions to check understanding and back up any verbal information with relevant handouts. Using pauses when speaking can be useful; this gives time for learners to assimilate new knowledge and ask questions if necessary. Using visual aids enables learners to see what you are expressing verbally. Remember to incorporate all the different learning styles during your teaching.

Working with individuals, and small and large groups

When you are teaching a group, you must accept that this is a collection of individuals, all with different needs and wants, and it's up to you to address these while keeping focused on the subject or topic of learning. Make sure you include everyone, either during activities or when asking questions. Your learners will probably be from different backgrounds and different age groups, have different skills, knowledge and experiences, but will all expect to learn something from you. Having some prior knowledge of your learners, gained from initial assessment, or by talking to them, will help ensure your sessions are effective.

Individuals often act differently depending upon the situation and the other people they are with at the time. How you act towards your learners may also change depending upon the context or circumstances you are teaching in. Different issues will arise when teaching individuals, as opposed to groups; it takes practice to give each individual the attention they need, while teaching the subject and controlling a group. This should all come with experience and it may benefit you to observe an experienced teacher who is teaching a large group.

Berne's (1973) *Transactional Analysis theory* is a method of analysing communications between people. Berne identified three personality states; the *child*, the *parent* and the *adult*. These states are called *ego states* and people behave and exist in a mixture of these states, depending on their past experiences and the situation at the time. The different states are manifest in gestures, vocal tones, expressions, attitudes, and vocabulary.

Transactional analysis assumes all past events, feelings and experiences are stored within, and can be re-experienced in current situations. You may see this with learners who take on a different state – for example, acting like a child asking for help – in a different situation with a different learner or teacher.

Transactions are verbal exchanges between two people: one speaks and the other responds. If the conversation is complementary then the transactions enable the conversation to continue. If the transactions are crossed, the conversation may change its nature or come to an end.

Berne recognised that people need *stroking*. Strokes are acts of recognition which one person gives to another. These can be physical, or verbal, as with words of appreciation, and strokes can be positive or negative. Giving or receiving positive strokes develops emotionally healthy people who are confident in themselves and have a feeling of being *okay*.

Example

Colin was working towards a recognised joinery qualification and wanted to prove how good he was, as well as please the teacher. He kept saying to himself, 'I'll be okay if I don't make mistakes and can please my teacher'. By doing this, Colin felt he would be looked upon more favourably and receive strokes of approval, which would encourage and motivate him.

Understanding a little about the different states of the child, parent and adult will help you see how learners, or indeed colleagues, take on different roles in different situations.

If you ever feel like a *child* at work, it may be because your manager is operating in their *parent* mode and you are responding in your *child* mode. Your *child* makes you feel small, afraid, undervalued, demotivated and rebellious. These feelings may make you undermine, withdraw, gossip, procrastinate, plot revenge or attempt to please in order to be rewarded. In this *child* mode, you cannot become a successful professional.

If you are in a managerial role at work, you may find yourself acting like a *parent*. You may have learned this from your parents' responses to you years ago. The *parent* mode makes you feel superior, detached and impatient. Being in this state can make you harden your tone, not listen to people, shout, bribe others into complying, and criticise them more than you appreciate them.

The best option is to be in the *adult* state. As an *adult*, you feel good about yourself, respectful of the talents and lives of others, delighted with challenges, proud of accomplishments and expectant of success. These feelings make you respond to others by appreciating and listening to them, using respectful language, perceiving the facts, considering alternatives and having a long-term view and enjoyment of work and life.

If you realise that you have moved into a *role*, it is possible to change if you need to.

When you feel your *child mode* about to make you withdraw, gossip or undermine, you can choose instead to participate, find out the facts and resolve your differences in the *adult* state.

When you feel your *parent mode* about to make you criticise, threaten, bribe or take over, you can choose instead to speak warmly, be patient, listen and find enjoyment in the challenge.

It is very difficult to be consistently in the *adult* state. You may find yourself adapting to different situations and responding to the states that other people have taken on.

There are transactions between people which can be destructive to at least one person, and these are called *games*. Games will leave someone feeling *not okay*. People play games for rewards, and they reinforce a particular life position, pass time and avoid the need to spend it more constructively.

Games can occur when someone suddenly switches out of the *adult* state. One game is called 'see *what you made me do*'.

Example

This is what happens when one person asks another for advice.

Rashid: 'Sarah, could you tell me what you think of this memo I've written?'

Sarah: 'Of course. I think it's fine, except I'd make the second sentence a bit more direct.'

Both people are operating adult to adult, known as a parallel transaction.

The game begins the next day when Rashid switches to his child state after hearing that the memo was considered offensive because the second sentence was too blunt.

Rashid: 'Thanks to you, I'm in trouble now.' (See what you made me do.)

The adult to adult transaction has become child to adult, known as a crossed transaction.

Having an awareness of the different states of child, parent and adult, you can observe how your learners are behaving and if necessary coax them into a more appropriate state. You may also notice yourself taking on different states, depending upon who you are with and the situation at the time.

Working as part of a team, or with groups, can also lead to communication problems. Dr Meredith Belbin (1993) defined team roles as: *A tendency to behave, contribute and interrelate with others in a particular way.*

Belbin's research identified nine clusters of behaviour, and each cluster defines a particular *team-role*. Each team-role embodies a combination of strengths which the role contributes to the team, as well as allowable weaknesses. For full details see the Belbin Team-Role Descriptions table on page 81.

The team-roles are grouped into *action, people* and *cerebral*:

- action-oriented roles: Shaper, Implementer, and Completer Finisher;

- people-oriented roles: Co-ordinator, Teamworker and Resource Investigator;

- cerebral roles: Plant, Monitor Evaluator and Specialist.

Sometimes teams become problematic, not because their members don't know their subject, but because they have problems accepting, adjusting and communicating with each other as they take on different roles. Knowing that individuals within teams take on these different roles will help you manage group work more effectively; for example, by grouping a mixture of the *action, people* and *cerebral* roles within each group.

Belbin® Team-Role Summary Descriptions

Team-Role Descriptions

Team Role	Contribution	Allowable Weakness
Plant	Creative, imaginative, unorthodox. Solves difficult problems.	Ignores incidentals. Too pre-occupied to communicate effectively.
Resource Investigator	Extrovert, enthusiastic, communicative. Explores opportunities. Develops contacts.	Over-optimistic. Loses interest once initial enthusiasm has passed.
Co-ordinator	Mature, confident, a good chairperson. Clarifies goals, promotes decision-making, delegates well.	Can be seen as manipulative. Offloads personal work.
Shaper	Challenging, dynamic, thrives on pressure. The drive and courage to overcome obstacles.	Prone to provocation. Offends people's feelings.
Monitor Evaluator	Sober, strategic and discerning. Sees all options. Judges accurately.	Lacks drive and ability to inspire others.
Teamworker	Co-operative, mild, perceptive and diplomatic. Listens, builds, averts friction.	Indecisive in crunch situations.
Implementer	Disciplined, reliable, conservative and efficient. Turns ideas into practical actions.	Somewhat inflexible. Slow to respond to new possibilities.
Completer Finisher	Painstaking, conscientious, anxious. Searches out errors and omissions. Delivers on time.	Inclined to worry unduly. Reluctant to delegate.
Specialist	Single-minded, self-starting, dedicated. Provides knowledge and skills in rare supply.	Contributes on only a narrow front. Dwells on technicalities.

www.belbin.com   © e-interplace®, Belbin Associates, UK. 1991-2006+

Coverdale (1977) states that the essence of team working is that individuals have their own preferred ways of achieving a task, but that in a team, they need to decide on one way of achieving this. In a team, three overlapping and interacting circles of needs have to be focused upon at all times: the *task needs*, the *team needs* and the *individual needs*.

When setting tasks or activities for learners to carry out in groups, consider the following:

To achieve the task, ensure:

- a SMART objective or target is stated;
- responsibilities are defined;
- working conditions are suitable;
- supervision is available.

To build and maintain the team, ensure:

- the size of the team is suitable for the task;
- health and safety factors are considered;
- consultation takes place;
- discipline and order are maintained.

To develop the individual, ensure:

- responsibilities are defined;
- grievances are dealt with;
- praise is given;
- learners feel safe and secure.

Individual personalities and the roles that learners take on when part of a group, may impede the successful achievement of the task. As a teacher, make sure you supervise group work carefully to keep all individuals focused and included.

Managing behaviour and disruption

Behaviour and disruption may occur if your learners are not self-motivated, challenged or stimulated to learn. You can help to create a climate which will encourage learning to take place. However, if disruptive situations arise, you will have to deal with them promptly, otherwise they could lead to further disruption which will hinder effective learning. Unfortunately, there isn't room within this book to cover all the information you might need throughout your teaching career. However, there are many relevant textbooks; for example, *Managing Behaviour in the Lifelong Learning Sector* (Wallace 2007), that can help you.

If you are teaching post-compulsory learners, they will probably be self-motivated and have a good attitude towards their learning. This in turn can be rewarding for you. However, adults can still be disruptive if they are not challenged enough or don't feel their learning is relevant. If you are teaching learners in the compulsory sector, they may have issues or problems which they bring to your sessions. They may be immature, causing them to arrive late, talk among themselves, send text messages or just appear uninterested. Sadly, it is a rare privilege to teach a group of motivated, interested learners and it falls upon you to manage and control the situation you are presented with, however exasperating, otherwise it will get out of hand. Finding suitable ways of dealing with disruption as it occurs will lead to an effective learning environment. This will come mainly from experiencing such situations and finding your own way of dealing with them. Observing experienced teachers will enable you to witness a variety of situations and see how others manage them.

Activity

Note down, after each session you teach, aspects of disruption that occurred and how you dealt with them. Write down how you felt at the time and what else was going on in the room. If similar kinds of disruption are happening repeatedly, consider different ways of responding to them and ask colleagues for advice.

As a teacher, you need to engage the attention of your learners at the beginning of the session. You can do this by ensuring that they are all on time and settled, before you state your aim. Being organised, having a detailed session plan, relevant resources and working equipment will help. If you make clear to your learners that you will always start on time, they will try their best to be there; if they see that you don't mind waiting for them, they won't make the effort. If you have learners who can't help arriving a few minutes late, perhaps because they are moving from another part of the building, or have work commitments, then a *starter activity* could be useful. This can involve a short group discussion based around the last session which recaps key points, or you can discuss the topic of the current session. It could even be a short multi-choice quiz that you have prepared earlier, to test their knowledge of the subject so far. In any case, it's always useful to have activities like this handy should you finish a session earlier than planned. Don't allow the group simply to talk amongst themselves while you wait for everyone to arrive; this could lead to a lack of attention by the time everyone is present. If you are delivering a one-off session, you could ask the group what they hope to learn from the session. You may find that your learners' expectations are different from what you plan to teach. Knowing what your learners are hoping for will enable you to address their needs, or at least explain why you won't be covering certain aspects. Your learners will then know what to expect, and will be less likely to leave your session feeling disappointed or let down.

Setting a few ground rules will help establish the boundaries for an effective session. Giving the learners ownership of these should help to ensure that they are maintained, and minimise disruption.

If you are passionate about your subject, this should help enthuse and motivate your learners. Keep your sessions active, involve your learners and build their self-esteem; ask relevant questions, use eye contact, use their names and give positive praise and feedback. Any subject can be made interesting to your learners; it's all about the way you choose to teach it. A session is boring to the learners only if the teacher delivers it in a boring way. If you are not interested, or don't prepare your materials adequately, your learners will lose confidence in you, begin to lack motivation, and the result will be disruption.

You can probably recall attending a session in the past, perhaps at school or college, where the teacher was really enthusiastic about the subject, and made the session interesting, enabling you to enjoy and learn in a comfortable atmosphere. Equally so, you have probably attended a session delivered by a teacher who was badly organised or lacked confidence, causing you to lose interest. Wherever possible, recognise the individual differences and experiences of your learners, encourage interaction between them and empower them; if they are mature enough, give them responsibility for their own learning. Having positive expectations of your learners and encouraging them to accomplish tasks, even if this is in small stages, will help them to see their progress and achievement.

Never lose your temper, embarrass your learners in front of their peers, or make disparaging comments about other learners, colleagues or the organisation within which you work; this is very unprofessional. Your learners need to feel good about their teacher, about themselves and their learning, and you can help this with the environment you create and the experiences you give your learners. (A sense of humour also helps!) You want your learners to return to your sessions keen to learn and to participate. Penalising bad behaviour; for example, by disallowing a break, asking a learner to stay behind, moving a learner to another seating position or issuing extra homework, may be effective with younger learners, but it's harder to challenge an adult, particularly if they are older than you. You need to get to know your learners to find out why they are being disruptive. Then address the cause of the problem, instead of generating further bad feeling. It's better to create order in a *pro-active* way within the group, by finding strategies that work for you all, than to impose order in a *reactive* way upon them.

It may help to ask your learners what they want from an effective teacher. If they feel that you are giving them what they want, their attitude towards their learning may be more positive. Don't ever take anything personally from a disruptive learner, or rise to an argument; it's usually the situation, not you, that has caused the problem. Changing the way the learner feels about the situation should help their attitude and prevent disruption in the future.

At the end of your sessions, ensure that you recap all relevant points and ask some questions, or have a quiz to check knowledge. You could give *points* for successful answers that can be added up throughout the course, and give a prize at the end to the learner with the most points. Some learners are motivated by friendly competition and achievement. Introduce the topic of the next session (if applicable), to give the learners something to look forward to.

Motivation

As a teacher, it's crucial to motivate your learners; to create in them a desire to learn. You must be enthusiastic and passionate about your subject; only then will you be able to inspire, stimulate and challenge your learners. They may already be motivated for personal reasons and be enthusiastic and keen to learn. This *wanting to learn for its own sake* comes from within. It is known as *intrinsic motivation*.

However, learners may be motivated to learn for other reasons, such as to gain a qualification, promotion or pay rise at work, or to attend because they need to in order to receive their training allowance. This is known as *extrinsic motivation,* which addresses an external *need* to learn. If you can recognise the difference between your learners' *wants* and *needs*, you can see why they are motivated, and can ensure that you make their learning meaningful and relevant. Learners who don't have intrinsic motivation may require encouragement to learn. They must have a *need* to learn as well as want to learn, and you may have to promote this desire within them by creating a climate of learning that is relevant, interesting and exciting.

Whatever type of motivation your learners bring to their first session with you, it will be transformed, for better or worse, by what happens during their learning experience.

Activity

Think about why you are reading this textbook. It must be for some reason. Is that reason because you want to learn something new? Or is it because you need to gain knowledge to achieve a qualification?

You probably want to learn something new as well as achieve a qualification. If this is the case, you have internal and external motivation, ensuring that you are keen to learn and have the desire to achieve.

Many factors can affect a learner's motivation to work and to learn; some may lack self-confidence, or have previous experiences of learning that were not successful. Therefore you need to ensure that you treat all learners as individuals, using their names and creating an interest in the subject matter, to help retain their motivation. Setting clear targets, ensuring activities are interesting and relevant, encouraging your learners to ask questions, and giving constructive and positive feedback will also help. Some learners may need more attention than others, but take care not not to neglect those who are progressing well; they still need encouragement and feedback to know they are on the right track. You also need a positive attitude towards the subject and the learning environment. You may not be able to change the type of environment you are teaching in, or the resources you are using. Nevertheless, remaining professional and making the best of what you have will help encourage learning to take place.

Learners may already have some knowledge or experience of the subject. In that case, you could incorporate time within your sessions to encourage discussions, paired or group work, to enhance their learning experience. Learners do like to talk about their own experiences, and others in the group may gain from these. You also need to acknowledge any limitations in your own knowledge and experience. You can improve or update this by taking part in professional development.

Encourage and motivate your learners to reach their maximum potential. If you set tasks that are too hard, learners may struggle and become frustrated and anxious. If tasks are too easy, learners may become bored. Knowing your learners and differentiating for their needs will help you to keep them motivated.

Your learners may already have a desire to learn for their own fulfilment or benefit, but still need motivating during your sessions, perhaps to pay attention, focus on tasks or take part in activities. Some learners may be attending your sessions as a requirement of training or employment, and may not really want to be there. If you can make the learning experience relevant to each learner by making it reflect, as closely as possbile, real-life scenarios, this should help them pay attention and remain motivated to learn. Creating a *what's in it for me?* culture, where learners create their own desire to learn, supported by your desire to teach them, will help their motivation.

Example

Sahib was having problems with a group of 14 learners in the computer room. Some would talk over him, use programmes not relevant to the session and use their mobile phones. He decided to spend a few minutes at the beginning of the next session asking each learner in turn (in front of the rest of the group) to state a reason for using a computer, that they could relate to in their personal or working life. He also asked the group to agree some ground rules which included switching off their mobile phones. This helped the learners see the relevance of various computer skills, enabling them to be more focused during the sessions.

Try and create an environment of respect, between learners and towards you. Whenever possible, give them responsibility for making decisions regarding their own learning needs.

If you have learners who are quite motivated already, keep this motivation alive with regular challenges and constructive and positive feedback. It also helps to keep in mind the different learning styles of your learners, and try to reach these.

Don't forget that the learning environment you create should meet your learners' basic needs, such as feeling safe and comfortable. Make sure that the room is at a comfortable temperature and adequately ventilated. Tell learners when the break will be, so that they know when they will be able to obtain refreshments. This all helps them to feel more relaxed and secure enough to learn and progress further.

As a teacher, you should always begin by carrying out an icebreaker to enable learners to feel at ease with the group and the environment. Negotiating and setting ground rules will also help the group to bond and understand the boundaries within which they are to work. Team-building activities can be used to raise motivation, perhaps after a lunch break or at the beginning of an evening session. Rewards, such as positive praise, points, prizes, medals or a trophy can also motivate learners in the right context.

Activity

Think back to an event you attended recently. Were you tired, hungry, too hot or too cold? Did you feel uncomfortable because you didn't know anyone else there? Did these factors affect your learning? If so, you were probably thinking about these rather than concentrating on the reason you were at the event. Did the facilitator do anything to alleviate these issues; did they even ask you if you had any concerns?

To gain attention, always state your aim clearly and ensure that your learners know what is expected of them. You could ask each learner to state how they feel they could use their new knowledge or skills. Explain what they will gain from the experience; for example, the ability to pass an assignment or test, and always give positive and developmental feedback.

Creating a motivated learning environment can lead to improved communication and enable successful learning to take place.

This chapter contributes towards the following minimum core elements (see Appendix 2 for cross-references):

L1, L2, L3, L6, L8, LS1, LS3, LL1, LR1, LR2, LR3, LW1, LW2, LW3;
PLS1, PLS2, PLS3, PLS4, PLL1, PLW1, PLW2, PLW3, PLW4;
NC1, NC2, NP1, NP2, NP3,
PNC3, PNC5, PNP8;
ICT3, ICTC1, ICTC2, ICTPC1, ICTPC2, ICTPC3, ICTPC4, ICTPC5.

Summary

In this chapter you have learnt about:

- communication skills;

- verbal and non-verbal communication;

- working with individuals, and small and large groups;

- managing behaviour and disruption;

- motivation.

References and further information

Belbin M (1993) *Team Roles At Work*, Oxford: Elsevier Science & Technology.

Berne E (1973) *Games People Play: The Psychology of Human Relationships*, London: Penguin Books Ltd.

Coverdale R (1977) *Risk Thinking*, Bradford: The Coverdale Organisation.

Gravells A (2008) *Preparing to Teach in the Lifelong Learning Sector* (3rd edn), Exeter: Learning Matters.

Jackson P (1968) *Life in Classrooms*, London: Thomson Learning.

Maslow A (1987) *Motivation and Personality* (3rd revised edn), New York: Pearson Education Ltd.

Stewart I Joines V (1987) *TA Today: A new introduction to Transactional Analysis*, Kegworth: Lifespace Publishing.

Wallace S (2007) *Managing Behaviour in the Lifelong Learning Sector* (2nd edn) Exeter: Learning Matters.

Websites

Adult Student's Guide to Survival and Success – http://www.adultstudent.com/

Educational theory – www.businessballs.com

Team roles – www.belbin.com

Tuckman's group formation – http://www.businessballs.com/tuckmanformingstorming normingperforming.htm

6 REFLECTION, EVALUATION AND FEEDBACK, AND CONTINUING PROFESSIONAL DEVELOPMENT

Introduction

In this chapter you will learn about:

- reflection;

- evaluation and feedback;

- continuing professional development.

There are activities and examples to help assist your understanding of how to reflect on and develop your own practice, evaluate yourself and your programme, receive feedback and maintain your continuing professional development as a teacher.

Guidance to address the minimum core of literacy, language, numeracy and information and communication technology (ICT) is integrated throughout and referenced at the end of the chapter.

Chapter 7 contains useful pro formas you may wish to use.

This chapter contributes towards the following: *scope* (S), *knowledge* (K) and *practice* (P) aspects of the professional standards (A–F domains) for teachers, tutors and trainers in the Lifelong Learning Sector.

AS4, AS5, AS7, AK4.2, AK4.3, AK5.1, AK5.2, AK6.1, AK6.2, AK7.1, AK7.2, AK7.3, AP2.2, AP3.1, AP4.2, AP4.3, AP6.1, AP7.1, AP7.2, AP7.3;
BS2, BS3, BS4, BK2.6, BK2.7, BK3.2, BK3.5, BK4.1, BP2.6, BP2.7, BP3.2, BP3.3, BP3.4, BP4.1, BP5.2;
CS1, CS3, CS4, CK1.1, CK1.2, CK4.1, CK4.2, CP1.1, CP3.4, CP3.5, CP4.1;
DS3, DK3.1, DK3.2, DP2.1, DP3.1, DP3.2;
ES4, EK4.2, EP4.2;
FS3, FK3.1, FP3.1, FP4.2.

The standards can be accessed at: http://www.lluk.org.uk/documents/professional_standards_for_itts_020107.pdf

Reflection

When you look in a mirror, you will see your own reflection. You may look at yourself and think you want to change something; for example, what you are wearing, or you may choose not to change anything. Reflections in a mirror enable you to see with your eyes something you might want to change. Reflecting upon your teaching enables you to *think* about what you have done, how you did it and why you decided to do it a certain way, with a view to changing or improving it in the future. All reflection should lead to an improvement in practice.

There are many theories regarding reflective practice, some of which will be explained within this chapter. A straightforward method is to have the *experience*, then *describe* it, *analyse* it and *revise* it (EDAR). This method should help you think about what has happened and then consider ways of changing and/or improving it.

Experience → Describe → Analyse → Revise

EDAR (Gravells 2008)

- *Experience* – a significant event or incident you would like to change or improve.

- *Describe* – aspects such as *who* was involved, *what* happened, *when* it happened and *where* it happened.

- *Analyse* – consider the experience more deeply and ask yourself *how* it happened and *why* it happened.

- *Revise* – think about *how* you would do things differently if the same event happened again and then try this out if you have the opportunity.

A way of getting into the habit of reflective practice is to complete an ongoing journal. Try though not to write it like a conventional diary with a simple description of events; instead use EDAR to *reflect* upon the events. and your learning and development.

Activity

Think of the last session you taught, or even a session you have attended as a learner. Use the pro forma in Chapter 7 to reflect upon it.

When reflecting, you don't always have to write things down. Often, when you finish teaching, you will be thinking about your session afterwards, perhaps on your journey home. You might discuss it with colleagues and find they have had similar experiences to yours. Discussing events in this way can enhance your own experiences. Do remember though if you are talking about specific learners, to maintain confidentiality. You may need to learn to accept constructive criticism and feedback. Don't take any criticism personally; it's probably not you, but the situation, that will need to be changed.

Reflection should become a part of your everyday teaching; your session plan might have an evaluation section for you to note your strengths and areas for development after your delivery, to enable you to improve in the future. If so, just apply EDAR when completing it. Reflection enables you to look at things in detail that perhaps you would not ordinarily consider. There may be events you would not want to change or improve as you felt they went really well. If this is the case, reflect on *why* they went well and use these methods in future sessions. Reflection should become a habit; if you are not able to write a reflective journal, mentally run through the EDAR points when you have time. As you become more experienced at reflective practice, you will progress from thoughts like *I rushed the session because we spent too much time talking* or *I should have used a larger font in the handout* to aspects of more significance to your professional role as a teacher. You may realise you need further training or support in some areas before you feel confident to make changes.

Kolb (1984) proposed a four-stage continuous learning process. His theory suggests that without reflection, people would continue to make mistakes. When you are teaching, you may make mistakes; you should therefore consider *why* they happened and *what* you would do differently next time, putting your plans into practice when you have the opportunity.

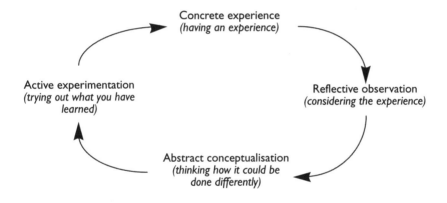

Kolb's (1984) Four-stage model of learning

This model of learning suggests that the cycle can be started at any stage; that reflection is as important as the experience; and that, once the cycle is started, it should be followed through all the stages for learning to be effective.

Example

Irene met her new group of learners on Monday evening. It was the first session of the programme and began with an icebreaker. Irene asked each learner to introduce themselves in front of the group. As the learners had never met, or been to the college before, they were nervous and the activity did not go well. After the session, Irene reflected upon the experience, considering how she could have done this differently, so with her next group, she tried a different icebreaker, which worked well.

Griffiths and Tann (1992) have further elaborated a model of reflection similar to Kolb's learning cycle by introducing different time frames. They state that, without a conscious effort, the most immediate reactions to experiences can overwhelm the opportunity for deeper consideration and learning. They describe the reflective cycle as:

action – observation – analysis – evaluation – planning

These go through five levels or time frames:

1. rapid reaction (immediate);

2. repair (short pause for thought);

3. review (time out to reassess, hours or days);

4. research (systematic, focused, weeks/months);

5. retheorise/reformulate (abstract, rigorous, over months/years).

There may be aspects of your teaching that will need time for changes or improvements to take effect. You might need to attend a training event, or devise new resources before you can try out these changes. You might teach a two-year programme and not have a chance to revisit the same session for another year, with a new group of learners. Reflection can therefore be immediate, i.e. after teaching a session, short term, if you teach the same session regularly, or medium/long term if not.

Ecclestone (1995) states that there is a danger of reflective practice becoming nothing more than a *mantra*, a comforting and familiar wrap, as opposed to a professional tool for exploration.

> *... people might also want – or need – reflection because they seek interest, inspiration, cultural breadth, critical analysis and reasoning, social insight and awareness, challenge and critique, or to create new knowledge.*
>
> Ecclestone (1995)

Reflective practice therefore implies a flexibility and a willingness to adapt, putting theory into practice.

Reflection can encompass:

● *a way of applying Kolb's learning cycle to reflect on and solve practical problems in the classroom;*

● *a focus for evaluating professional practice against external criteria;*

● *an in-depth and rigorous inquiry into professional practice, with a view to implementing change;*

● *a rare and much-needed chance to compare practice and problems through structured and supportive discussion with peers;*

- *an opportunity for disempowered complaining and negativity;*
- *an exchange of practical teaching hints.*

Ecclestone (1995:150)

You may be familiar with the term *critical incident analysis*. A critical incident is something you interpret as a problem or a challenge in a particular context, rather than a routine occurrence. An example of a critical incident is when learners repeatedly arrive late for a session. Critical incident analysis is a way of dealing with challenges in everyday situations, and exploring incidents that occur during your sessions in order to understand them better, and find alternative ways of reacting and responding to them.

Often, a critical incident is personal to an individual. Incidents become critical, that is, problematic, only if the individual sees them in this way. It is after the event that it is defined as critical. Carrying out a critical incident analysis can help you question your own practice and enable it to develop.

Example

Pablo has a group of 25 learners, eight of whom would always arrive five minutes late to the session. Pablo asked them why this happened and ascertained that they finished another class at the same time as this one was due to start. They therefore did not have enough time to move from one room to another without being late. Pablo arranged with the full group to start and finish the session slightly later. This enabled the group to be together at the beginning, minimising any disruption.

Tripp (1993) stated: *When something goes wrong, we need to ask what happened and what caused it to happen.* The guiding principle is to change the incident into a question. So, for example, *learners repeatedly arrive late for a session* changes to *why do learners repeatedly arrive late to my session?* In this way, critical incidents can become major turning points. Asking *why* enables you to work on the values of your professional practice.

Martin (1996) developed six aspects to critical incident analysis:

1 Choose a critical incident:
   this would be something that stands out for you; for example, a learner being disruptive.

2 Describe the incident to include:
   when and where it happened (time of day, location and context);
   what actually happened (who said or did what);
   what you were thinking and feeling at the time and just after the incident.

3 Interrogate your description to include:
why did this incident stand out?
what was going on?
did you have a personal bias or a particular mindset to the event?

4 Find a friend or colleague to:
share your account of the incident;
discuss your interpretation to see what you can learn from the incident and reach a resolution;
modify your analysis where necessary, in the light of peer feedback, to interpret the incident differently from another point of view.

5 Where appropriate, you may want to compare your analysis with the views of other key people involved in the episode (learners, colleagues, etc).

6 Write a report of the incident, maintaining confidentiality.

Activity

Think of a critical incident that has happened lately and work through the six points above to see if you can reach a solution.

You may find that these aspects work for you, or perhaps you prefer a different way of reflecting upon situations, such as that of Schön (1983). You may find that you just *do it* rather than *talking* or *writing* about it. Schön suggests:

- reflection in action;

- reflection on action.

Reflection *in action* is immediate and often unconscious, and happens at the time of the incident.

Example

Rachel was teaching a group of 16–19-year-olds; it was the second session of a 10-week programme. The group had gelled well during induction; however, they were quite noisy and took a while to calm down. Rachel had planned a practical activity, in small groups. She had asked the learners to nominate a person in each group to deliver a short presentation. This led to arguments as to who would or wouldn't give the presentation. Rachel immediately took control and nominated a learner within each group.

You will have prepared a session plan in advance of your teaching; however, you might not always follow this due to incidents within your session. You are a professional, and will react to situations as they happen, to meet the needs of your learners and maintain a positive learning environment. You may be teaching with equipment that could be a potential safety hazard; you would therefore stop using this as soon as a hazard becomes real. Reflection in action will come with experience.

Reflection *on action* takes place after the incident and is a more conscious process. This allows you time to think about the incident, considering a different approach, or to talk to others about it.

Example

Olaf was teaching English literature to a group of mature adults attending an evening class. The first half of the session went well, with learners discussing aspects of the key text they had covered during the previous session. After the break, Olaf introduced a new key text and read several paragraphs from it. The group were not familiar with the text and did not respond to Olaf's questions. He followed his session plan for the rest of the evening but his learners were not very enthusiastic. On his journey home, Olaf thought about why the learners were not enthusiastic about the new text. He realised he should have informed them the previous week about it, to give them a chance to research the author and subject, ready for discussion this week.

Often, taking time to reflect on your sessions, or incidents within them, enables you to plan different ways of doing things. Don't blame yourself if things don't go quite to your plan; it's all right to take risks sometimes and make impromptu changes to your session (as long as it's safe to do so). You can then consider afterwards why you did this and whether it worked or not. You always need to take into account your learners, what might work with one group may not work with another. Making changes comes with experience and knowledge.

Try not to blame others for incidents that happen within your sessions; you are the teacher in control, and must take responsibility. If you shift the blame onto others, you may feel there is no need to make any changes yourself. Don't necessarily blame yourself either, but do accept responsibility, learn from the incidents and try different methods to ensure they don't happen again. (Conversely, when a session goes well, reward yourself with praise and keep up your good practice.)

It will depend upon the incident as to how you react and reflect upon it. Reflective theories are very similar and you may even decide on your own model of reflection to help you improve your practice. Keeping a reflective learning journal will help you plan aspects for your continuing professional development (CPD).

Evaluation and feedback

Evaluating yourself, your teaching and your group's learning will help to improve your practice in the future. Whether you deliver a one-day programme, evening classes, or a full-time programme, you need to evaluate the process and gain feedback from your learners. This enables them to have a say in their learning. Ultimately, your evaluation of their contribution will result in a better service to your learners – think of it as *customer satisfaction*. Feedback helps you to identify any issues, or problems that can be overcome. Sometimes improvements can be made simply by changing the wording of a handout or the way you ask questions.

Evaluate yourself after each session you teach, and consider what went well, and which aspects you would improve or change for the next time. You should also evaluate any resources or activities you use. If your learners are struggling with an activity you have given them, it could be that you didn't explain it fully; if you ask a question that a learner can't answer, it's possible that you phrased it in a way that was difficult for them to understand. If one learner doesn't understand something, others might not either.

Activity

After the next session you teach, write down what you felt went well, what you would improve or change next time, and how you would go about this.

Feedback – from your learners, or others you work with – is essential in order for you to evaluate your teaching. You might be observed by colleagues, curriculum managers or inspectors to ensure that effective learning is taking place. You will gain valuable feedback from this and should act on any aspects identified. If further training is recommended, don't take this personally; instead, appreciate how much it will improve your role professionally. You might also take part in your organisation's appraisal process; this will help you negotiate and plan your professional development. Some of your CPD may be supported by your organisation but if it is not, it is your responsibility to arrange it and keep an up-to-date record.

Feedback from learners can be obtained informally by individual or group discussions or formally by using questionnaires. Often, learners are pleased to have the opportunity to complete questionnaires, providing they have the time to do so; giving them anonymity will help obtain objective feedback. Try to include time towards the end of a session for learners to fill in questionnaires; otherwise, if you ask them to complete one in their own time, they might not all return them. If you are teaching a longer programme, perhaps over two or three terms, it's best to obtain feedback part of the way through. You then have time to make any relevant changes during the programme. Never make assumptions that the programme is going well, just because you think it is.

When asking questions or designing questionnaires, you need to be careful of the type of questions you are using. Will these be closed, i.e. a question requiring only a *yes* or *no* answer; will they be multiple choice, enabling the learner to choose one or more responses to a question; or will they be open, leading to detailed responses?

Example

'Did the programme meet your expectations? YES/NO'

This closed question would not help you understand why the programme met the learners' expectations, or even what their expectations were. This would be better phrased: 'How did the programme meet your expectations?' This open question encourages the learners to answer in detail and gives you something to act on.

If you use closed or multiple-choice questions, you can add up how many responses you gained, to give you *quantitative* data. Other responses will give you *qualitative* data. Quantitative data is useful for obtaining statistics, but will not give you much information to help you improve specific aspects of your programme. Although you can add up the responses quickly from quantitative data, qualitative data is more useful. You might find it best to use a mixture of open and closed questions, but be careful with your wording of these to enable you to obtain information which will help you to make improvements. When designing questionnaires, use the KISS method – keep it short and simple. Don't overcomplicate your questions, for instance, by asking two questions in one sentence, or make the questionnaire so long that learners will not want to complete it. Explain to your learners why you are asking them to complete this questionnaire, and what the information will be used for. Always make sure you act on the results and feedback you receive, otherwise the evaluation process is meaningless.

Activity

Design a short questionnaire that you could use with your learners. Consider the types of questions you will ask, based upon the information you need. If possible, use this with a group of learners, analyse the results and recommend improvements to be made based on these.

Searching the internet will give you lots of ideas to help you design your questionnaire.

To evaluate your group's learning, you will need data such as success rates and examination results, or feedback from your learners' employers if their learning contributes to their job role. Funding providers, inspectors and your managers often need statistics to evaluate the success of programmes and determine whether they should be offered again. These statistics will probably be based on numbers of learners starting (known as *starters*) and completing the programme (known as *retention*), as well as those that achieved a qualification (known as *achievement*). You may have been given targets and, if these are not met, the programme may not be offered again in the future.

Example

Jenny taught a group of learners aiming to achieve an NVQ in Customer Service. She recruited 18 starters to the programme, which was her target figure. However, six subsequently withdrew, leaving a group of 12. Nine learners achieved the qualification. As a result, the programme had a 66% retention rate and a 75% achievement rate. These figures were lower than her targets of 90% and 80% respectively, meaning the programme would not be offered again.

Careful interviewing and initial assessments will help to ensure that learners are on the right programme.

Continuing professional development

Initial professional development (IPD) begins in teacher training if you are not already qualified or are currently working towards a qualification; continuing professional development (CPD) is required yearly for all teachers, trainers and tutors employed in the Lifelong Learning Sector, who must complete 30 hours on a pro-rata basis according to the hours they teach.

The 2007 regulations regarding CPD complement the Institute for Learning's (IfL) aim to promote teacher-centred development activities:

> *CPD, in relation to a teacher, means continuing professional development, which is any activity undertaken for the purposes of updating knowledge of the subject taught and developing teaching skills.*
>
> www.ifl.ac.uk

In this definition, CPD is fundamental in maintaining the good professional standing of all teachers in the sector and is the mechanism through which high-quality learning opportunities for the individual professional and the institution are identified, maintained and developed.

As a teacher and a professional, you need to continually update your skills and knowledge. This knowledge relates not only to your subject specialism, but also to teaching methods, the types of learners you will be teaching and relevant institutional and national policies. It can be formal or informal, planned well in advance or be opportunistic. CPD should have a real impact upon your job role and lead to an improvement in your practice.

CPD is more than just attending programmes; it's also about using critical reflection to evaluate your experiences in order to facilitate your development as a teacher. Experiences such as shadowing colleagues to observe their teaching, having a mentor, and support from your peers will all help your development.

When you are deciding upon activities to maintain your CPD, don't think only about attending programmes; ask yourself what would be most effective for devel-

oping yourself as a professional teacher, leading to an improvement in your job role, and ultimately impacting on your learners. Ways to do this can include:

- attending events, exhibitions and conferences;
- attending meetings and standardisation activities, and making a significant input;
- e-learning activities;
- evaluating feedback;
- joining professional associations or committees;
- peer observations,
- research;
- researching developments or changes to your subject and/or legislation;
- secondments;
- self-reflecting;
- subscribing to relevant journals;
- taking further qualifications;
- team-teaching;
- visits to other organisations;
- voluntary work;
- writing or reviewing books and articles;

and anything else that is realistic and relevant to your teaching role.

You can update your CPD via the IfL website (www.ifl.ac.uk). By now you should have registered as a member and you will have access to a wealth of information concerning ways to maintain your CPD.

When planning your CPD, it's best to complete a *personal development plan*. This enables you to consider your development needs and the best way to achieve them; they should relate directly to your job role or subject specialism.

Activity

Access the IfL website (www.ifl.ac.uk) and look at their model for CPD. Consider these aspects to help you decide what CPD activities you will undertake. If you can't access the website, consider what CPD you feel is relevant to you. You could use the personal development plan pro forma in Chapter 7 to formalise this.

Having the support of your organisation will help you decide what is relevant to your development as a teacher and to your job role.

The IfL states:

> The activities you choose as relevant to you and your practice will only count as CPD if:
>
> - you can critically reflect on what you have learned;
> - you can evidence how you have applied this to your practice;
> - you can evidence how this has impacted on your learners' experience and success.

Don't become complacent and dismiss the idea of further training as too time-consuming; be positive and treat it as a new challenge. To be a good teacher, you need dedication, commitment, motivation, enthusiasm and a passion for your subject. If you can exhibit all these qualities while teaching, you will help motivate your learners. However, there may be other barriers to your development besides time, such as finance, resources, or travel issues. If so, discuss these with your Human Resources department to see if help is available. You may be able to get a grant from your local authority to take higher level qualifications.

To achieve Associate or Qualified teacher status in the Learning and Skills Sector (ATLS/QTLS) you will need to evidence your CPD yearly.

The IfL will monitor CPD each year to ensure you achieve the required minimum amount of hours.

Example

Laurence teaches hairdressing in a training organisation for two and a half days a week and is currently taking the Certificate in Teaching in the Lifelong Learning Sector. He is required to maintain his skills as a hairdresser by working in a salon, which he does on a regular basis. He is also a member of the relevant hairdressing associations and reads hairdressing journals and magazines regularly. He is therefore more than meeting his required CPD hours.

You will probably have a mentor to support you while you are working towards your teaching qualification. He or she should be qualified in your subject area to give specific advice and support. You could observe their teaching to gain new insights into the teaching of your subject and give you new or different ideas to help improve your own teaching.

Activity

Using the observation checklist in Chapter 7, arrange to observe your mentor, or another colleague in the same subject area, teaching a session. You can then reflect upon the experience to help improve your own practice.

You might attend standardisation events which give you the opportunity to compare your delivery, resources and assessment decisions with colleagues. Even if you don't learn anything new, such events will confirm that you are doing things correctly.

You will also probably take part in an appraisal system in your organisation. This is a valuable opportunity to discuss your learning and any training or support you may need in the future. Always keep a copy of any documentation relating to your training and CPD, as you may need to provide this to funding, Awarding/Examining bodies or regulatory authorities if requested.

The IfL has a Code of Professional Practice which all members should abide by. This Code defines the professional behaviour which, in the public interest, the IfL expects of its members throughout their membership and professional career. The IfL will maintain and update its standards of professional conduct, ensuring continued public confidence. As a member of the IfL you will need to recognise your ongoing obligations.

Activity

Have a look at the IfL Code of Professional Practice on their website, www.ifl.ac.uk, and consider your obligations towards this.

Change is inevitable in education; therefore, it's crucial to keep up to date with any developments regarding your subject specialism, and with relevant legislation. For example, if you are not very competent at using a computer, or your maths and English need to be improved, you will have to do something about this.

Activity

Access www.move-on.org.uk, register your details and work through the maths or English activities. Or carry out a search via the internet for other relevant sites to help improve your skills.

Reflecting upon your own teaching, taking account of feedback from learners and colleagues, then evaluating your practice and maintaining your professional development, will enable you to become an effective and proficient teacher. This will lead to a rewarding career for yourself and a worthwhile future for your learners.

This chapter contributes towards the following minimum core elements (see Appendix 2 for cross-references):

L1, L2, L3, L4, L7, L8, LS1, LS2, LS3, LL1, LR1, LR2, LR3, LW1, LW2, LW3; PLS1, PLS2, PLS3, PLS4, PLL1, PLR1, PLR2, PLR3, PLW1, PLW2, PLW3, PLW4;
N1, N2, N3, NC1, NC2, NP1, NP2, NP3, NP5, NP6;
PNC1, PNC2, PNC3, PNC4, PNC5, PNP1, PNP2, PNP3, PNP4, PNP5, PNP6, PNP7, PNP8;
ICT1, ICT2, ICT5, ICTC1, ICTP1, ICTPC2, ICTPC3, ICTPC5, ICTPP1, ICTPP2, ICTPP3

Summary

In this chapter you have learnt about:

- reflection;

- evaluation and feedback;

- continuing professional development.

References and further information

Ecclestone K (1995) The Reflective Practitioner: Mantra or Model for Emancipation, *Studies in the Education of Adults*, Vol 28, No 2.

Gravells A (2008) *Preparing to Teach in the Lifelong Learning Sector* (3rd edn), Exeter: Learning Matters.

Griffiths M and Tann S (1992) Using reflective practice to link personal and public theories, *Journal of Education for Teaching*, Vol 18, No 1.

Hitching J (2008) *Maintaining Your Licence to Practise*, Exeter: Learning Matters.

Jackson P (2004) Understanding the experience of experience: a practical model of reflective practice for coaching, *International Journal of Evidence Based Coaching and Mentoring*, Vol 2, No 1.

Kolb D A (1984) *Experiential Learning: Experience as the Source for Learning and Development*, New Jersey: Prentice-Hall.

Martin K (1996) Critical Incidents in Teaching and Learning, *Issues of Teaching and Learning*, Vol 2, No 8.

Schön D (1983) *The Reflective Practitioner*, San Francisco: Jossey-Bass.

Tripp D (1993) *Critical Incidents in Teaching: Developing Professional Judgement*, London: Routledge.

Tummons J (2007) *Becoming a Professional Tutor in the Lifelong Learning Sector*, Exeter: Learning Matters.

Websites

English and maths online tests – www.move-on.org.uk

Further Education Teachers' Qualifications (England) Regulations 2007, no 2264 – http://www.opsi.gov.uk/si/si2007/uksi_20072264_en_1

Institute for Learning – www.ifl.ac.uk

Lifelong Learning UK – www.lluk.org.uk

Post Compulsory Education & Training Network – www.pcet.net

7 SAMPLE DOCUMENTATION

This chapter contains sample documents referred to within the chapters, which you may like to use in preparation for, or as part of, your teaching role. They are examples only, and can be adapted to suit your own requirements. If you are currently teaching or taking a qualification, your organisation will already have certain documents they will require you to use, which may differ from these.

> The documents (listed below) are also available from the publisher's website, www.learningmatters.co.uk
>
> - Continuing professional development record
> - Individual learning plan/action plan
> - Induction checklist
> - Initial assessment record
> - Observation checklist
> - Personal development plan
> - Programme evaluation
> - Reflective learning journal
> - Scheme of work
> - Session plan
> - Tutorial review

Continuing professional development record

Name:

Organisation:

IfL number:

Date	Activity	Venue	Duration	Justification towards teaching role/subject specialism	Further training needs	Evidence Ref Number e.g. personal reflections, notes, certificates etc

Individual learning plan/action plan

Name:

Programme/qualification:

Start date:

Teacher:

Expected achievement date:

Venue:

Programme/qualification aims:

Results of initial assessments, skills scan and learning styles tests:

Special assessment requirements or support that may be required:

Action plan

Learning goals	Functional Skills	Target date	Achievement date

Personal/other goals	Target date	Achievement date

Reviews/updates to plan

Date	Learner comments	Teacher comments

Signed (learner):

Signed (teacher):

Induction checklist

Organisation

- [ ] an introduction to the organisation, for example, mission statement;
- [ ] who's who within the staff, i.e. names, roles, responsibilities;
- [ ] where to go for help and advice;
- [ ] policies and procedures, for example, health and safety, security;
- [ ] evacuation procedures/first aid in case of an emergency;
- [ ] what learners can expect from the organisation;
- [ ] what you expect from learners;
- [ ] methods of communication, for example, telephone, e-mail;
- [ ] procedures to follow in case of absence or lateness;
- [ ] enrolment/form filling procedures.

Programme

- [ ] programme/qualification details and dates;
- [ ] assessment details;
- [ ] coursework/homework;
- [ ] appeals and complaints procedures;
- [ ] provision for learning support;
- [ ] tutorial/review procedures;
- [ ] costs and methods of payment;
- [ ] access to hardship funds;
- [ ] commitment both during the programme and in learners' own time;
- [ ] available resources and how to access them;
- [ ] initial assessment requirements, for example, learning styles tests, literacy, numeracy and ICT tests;
- [ ] possible guests/visiting speakers/field trips;
- [ ] progression opportunities.

Facilities

- [ ] toilets, catering, parking, smoking;
- [ ] disabled access and facilities;
- [ ] crèche and childcare facilities;
- [ ] rooms and learning environments;
- [ ] computer and library facilities and access;
- [ ] opening and closing times;
- [ ] travel arrangements;
- [ ] access to an interpreter.

Initial assessment record

Name: **Date:**

Programme/qualification: **Venue:**

What relevant experience do you have?		
What relevant qualifications do you have?		
Have you completed a learning styles questionnaire? If YES, what is your preferred style of learning?	YES/NO	
Do you have any particular learning needs or special requirements? If YES, please state, or talk to your teacher in confidence.	YES/NO	
Are you confident at using a computer? If YES, what experience or qualifications do you have?	YES/NO	Skills Scan Results: ICT:
Do you feel you have a good command of written/spoken English?	YES/NO	Skills Scan Results: Literacy:
Do you feel your numeracy skills need improving?	YES/NO	Skills Scan Results: Numeracy:
Why have you decided to take this programme/qualification (*continue overleaf*)		

An individual learning plan should now be agreed.

Signed (learner):   Signed (teacher):

Observation checklist

Teacher: **Date:**

Observer: **Venue:**

Group: **Programme/qualification:**

Did the teacher... ?	Comments	Action required
Have a scheme of work (if applicable)		
Have a suitable session plan		
Prepare the venue and equipment in advance (adhering to health and safety requirements)		
Have adequate resources available		
State aims and objectives		
Establish and maintain a rapport with the learners		
Use a range of teaching and learning activities		
Encourage all learners to participate		
Communicate appropriately		
Ensure equality, entitlement, diversity, inclusion and differentiation		
Recap important points regularly		
Integrate functional skills into their delivery		
Demonstrate knowledge of own subject		
Demonstrate knowledge of the minimum core		
Deal with disruption as it occurred		
Ask questions to check knowledge		

Give appropriate feedback		
Enable learners to ask questions and give feedback		
Summarise the session		
Link to the next session (if applicable)		
Achieve their aim/objectives?		
Leave the venue clean and tidy		
Complete relevant records		
Evaluate their session afterwards		

Overall feedback:

Signed (teacher):   Signed (observer):

Personal development plan

Name:

Organisation:

Timescale	Aims	Costs involved/ organisational support	Start date	Review date	Completion date _CPD record to be updated_
Short term					
Medium term					
Long term					

Programme evaluation

Programme title: **Dates of programme:**

Teacher: **Venue:**

Please circle from 1–5
(1 is low/no, 5 is high/yes)

Did you receive thorough information, advice and guidance before starting your programme? 1 2 3 4 5

Was the programme content as you expected? 1 2 3 4 5

Were the handouts and activities helpful? 1 2 3 4 5

Were the delivery methods suitable? 1 2 3 4 5

Were the assessment methods suitable? 1 2 3 4 5

Were your questions dealt with adequately? 1 2 3 4 5

Was the teacher helpful and supportive? 1 2 3 4 5

Did the venue meet your expectations? 1 2 3 4 5

Did the facilities meet your expectations? 1 2 3 4 5

Did the programme meet your requirements? 1 2 3 4 5

Do you feel you have benefited from the programme? 1 2 3 4 5

Did you have access to expert advice and guidance on progression opportunities at the end of your programme? 1 2 3 4 5

Was there sufficient access to staff and materials outside of programme time? 1 2 3 4 5

Are there any changes you would recommend?

Further comments:

Learner name:
Leave blank if you wish

Date:

Reflective learning journal

Name: **Date:**

Experience *significant event or incident*	
Describe *who, what, when, where*	
Analyse *why, how (impact on teaching and learning)*	
Revise *changes and/or improvements required*	

Scheme of work

Teacher:

Programme/qualification	Group	Dates from:	to:
Number of sessions	Delivery hours	Venue	
Aim of programme			

Dates	Objectives	Activities and resources	Assessment

Session plan

Teacher		Date		Venue	
Subject and level/ syllabus reference		Time and Duration		Number of learners	
Aim of session	*Integrate functional skills of English, maths and ICT where possible*				
Group composition	*Consider differentiation, individual learning needs and learning styles*				

Timing	Objectives	Resources	Teacher activities	Learner activities	Assessment

Self-evaluation

Strengths	Areas for development	Action and improvements required

Tutorial review

Teacher: **Date:**

Learner: **Venue:**

Issues discussed	
Progress and achievements	
Action required with target dates	

Signed (learner):   Signed (teacher):

ACCAC	Awdurdod Cymwysterau, Cwricwlwm ac Asesu Cymru/ Qualifications, Curriculum and Assessment Authority for Wales
ACL	Adult and Community Learning
ADS	Adult Dyslexia Support
ALN	Adult Literacy and Numeracy
APEL	Accreditation of Prior Experience and Learning
APL	Accreditation of Prior Learning
ATLS	Associate Teacher Learning and Skills
BSA	Basic Skills Agency
CCEA	Council for the Curriculum, Examinations and Assessment
CETT	Centre for Excellence in Teaching and Training
CGLI	City & Guilds of London Institute
CoVE	Centre of Vocational Excellence
CPD	Continuing Professional Development
CRE	Commission for Racial Equality
CTLLS	Certificate in Teaching in the Lifelong Learning Sector
DCFS	Department for Children, Families and Schools
DDA	Disability Discrimination Act
DELLS	Department for Education, Lifelong Learning and Skills
DIUS	Department for Innovation, Universities and Skills
DRC	Disability Rights Commission
DTLLS	Diploma in Teaching in the Lifelong Learning Sector
ELWA	Education and Learning Wales
EOC	Equal Opportunities Commission
ESOL	English for Speakers of Other Languages
EU	European Union
HSE	Health and Safety Executive
ICT	Information Communication Technology
IfL	Institute for Learning
ILP	Individual Learning Plan
ILT	Information Learning Technology

IT	Information Technology
ITT	Initial Teacher Training
IWB	Interactive Whiteboard
LAR	Learner Achievement Record
LLN	Language, Literacy, Numeracy
LLUK	Lifelong Learning UK
LSC	Learning and Skills Council
LSN	Learning and Skills Network
NIACE	National Institute of Adult Continuing Education
NQT	Newly Qualified Teacher
NVQ	National Vocational Qualification
Ofsted	Office for Standards in Education, Children's Services and Skills
OHP	Overhead projector
PCET	Post Compulsory Education and Training
PDR	Personal Development Record
PGCE	Post Graduate Certificate in Education
PTLLS	Preparing to Teach in the Lifelong Learning Sector
QAA	Quality Assurance Agency
QCA	Qualifications and Curriculum Authority
QCF	Qualification and Credit Framework
QIA	Quality Improvement Agency
QTLS	Qualified Teacher Learning and Skills
RARPA	Recognition and Recording of Progress and Achievement
SMART	Specific, Measurable, Achievable, Realistic, Timebound
SQA	Scottish Qualifications Authority
SSC	Sector Skills Council
SVUK	Standards Verification UK
TTA	Teacher Training Agency
VACSR	Valid, Authentic, Current, Sufficient, Reliable
VARK	Visual, Aural, Read/Write, Kinaesthetic
VLE	Virtual Learning Environment
VQ	Vocational Qualification
WBL	Work Based Learning
WWWWWH	Who, What, When, Where, Why and How

UNIT TITLE: Planning and enabling learning, level three (nine credits)

Learning outcomes The learner will:	Assessment criteria The learner can:
1 Understand ways to negotiate appropriate individual goals with learners	1.1 Explain the role of initial assessment in the learning and teaching process 1.2 Describe different methods of initial assessment for use with learners 1.3 Explain ways of planning, negotiating and recording appropriate learning goals with learners
2 Understand how to plan for inclusive learning	2.1 Establish and maintain an inclusive learning environment 2.2 Devise a scheme of work which meets learners' needs and curriculum requirements 2.3 Devise session plans which meet the aims and needs of learners 2.4 Explain ways in which session plans can be adapted to the individual needs of learners 2.5 Plan the appropriate use of a variety of delivery methods, explaining the choice 2.6 Identify opportunities for learners to provide feedback to inform practice
3 Understand how to use teaching and learning strategies and resources inclusively to meet curriculum requirements	3.1 Use a range of inclusive learning activities to enthuse and motivate learners, ensuring that curriculum requirements are met 3.2 Identify the strengths and limitations of a range of resources, including new and emerging technologies, showing how these resources can be used to promote equality, support diversity and contribute to effective learning 3.3 Identify literacy, language, numeracy and ICT skills which are integral to own specialist area 3.4 Select/adapt and use a range of inclusive resources to promote inclusive learning and teaching
4 Understand how to use a range of communication skills and methods to communicate effectively with learners and relevant parties in own organisation	4.1 Use different communication methods and skills to meet the needs of learners and the organisation 4.2 Identify ways in which own communication skills could be improved, including an explanation of how barriers to effective communication might be overcome 4.3 Liaise with other relevant parties to effectively meet the needs of learners

5 Understand and demonstrate knowledge of the minimum core in own practice	5.1 Apply minimum core specifications in literacy to improve own practice 5.2 Apply minimum core specifications in language to improve own practice 5.3 Apply minimum core specifications in mathematics to improve own practice 5.4 Apply minimum core specifications in ICT user skills to improve own practice
6 Understand how reflection, evaluation and feedback can be used to develop own practice	6.1 Use regular reflection and feedback from others, including learners, to evaluate and improve own practice

UNIT TITLE: Planning and enabling learning, level four (nine credits)

Learning outcomes The learner will:	Assessment criteria The learner can:
1 Understand ways to negotiate appropriate individual goals with learners	1.1 Analyse the role of initial assessment in the learning and teaching process 1.2 Describe and evaluate different methods of initial assessment for use with learners 1.3 Evaluate ways of planning, negotiating and recording appropriate learning goals with learners
2 Understand how to plan for inclusive learning	2.1 Establish and maintain an inclusive learning environment 2.2 Devise and justify a scheme of work which meets learners' needs and curriculum requirements 2.3 Devise and justify session plans which meet the aims and needs of individual learners and/or groups 2.4 Analyse ways in which session plans can be adapted to the individual needs of learners 2.5 Plan the appropriate use of a variety of delivery methods, justifying the choice 2.6 Identify and evaluate opportunities for learners to provide feedback to inform practice
3 Understand how to use teaching and learning strategies and resources inclusively to meet curriculum requirements	3.1 Select/adapt, use and justify a range of inclusive learning activities to enthuse and motivate learners, ensuring that curriculum requirements are met 3.2 Analyse the strengths and limitations of a range of resources, including new and emerging technologies, showing how these resources can be used to promote equality, support diversity and contribute to effective learning 3.3 Identify literacy, language, numeracy and ICT skills which are integral to own specialist area, reviewing how they support learner achievement 3.4 Select/adapt, use and justify a range of inclusive resources to promote inclusive learning and teaching

4 Understand how to use a range of communication skills and methods to communicate effectively with learners and relevant parties in own organisation	4.1 Use and evaluate different communication methods and skills to meet the needs of learners and the organisation 4.2 Evaluate own communication skills, identifying ways in which these could be improved, including an analysis of how barriers to effective communication might be overcome 4.3 Identify and liaise with appropriate and relevant parties to effectively meet the needs of learners
5 Understand and demonstrate knowledge of the minimum core in own practice	5.1 Apply minimum core specifications in literacy to improve own practice 5.2 Apply minimum core specifications in language to improve own practice 5.3 Apply minimum core specifications in mathematics to improve own practice 5.4 Apply minimum core specifications in ICT user skills to improve own practice
6 Understand how reflection, evaluation and feedback can be used to develop own good practice	6.1 Use regular reflection and feedback from others, including learners, to evaluate and improve own practice, making recommendations for modification as appropriate

Guidance for awarding institutions on teacher roles and initial teaching qualifications LLUK (2007)
Printed with permission from Lifelong Learning UK
The full document is available at: http://www.lluk.org.uk/documents/.uoa_all.pdf

Planning and enabling learning – professional standards for teachers, tutors and trainers in the lifelong learning sector

Planning and enabling learning, level three:	
Values and commitments included in the unit:	AS 1; AS 3; AS 4; BS 1; BS 2; BS 3; BS 4; BS 5; CS 1; CS 2; CS 3; DS 1; DS 2; ES 1; FS 1; FS 4
Standards included in the unit:	AK 1.1; AP 1.1; AK 3.1; AP 3.1; AK 4.2; AP 4.2; BK 1.1; BP 1.1; BK 1.2; BP 1.2; BK 2.1; BP 2.1; BK 2.2; BP 2.2; BK 2.3; BP 2.3; BK 2.4; BP 2.4; BK 2.5; BP 2.5; BK 2.6; BP 2.6; BK 3.1; BP 3.1; BK 3.2; BP 3.2; BK 3.3; BP 3.3; BK 3.4; BP 3.4; BK 3.5; BP 3.5; BK 4.1; BP 4.1; BK 5.1; BP 5.1; BK 5.2; BP 5.2; CK 1.1; CP 1.1; CK 2.1; CP 2.1; CK 3.1; CP 3.1; CK 3.2; CP 3.2; CK 3.3; CP 3.3;

	CK 3.4; CP 3.4; CK3.5; CP 3.5; DK 1.1; DP 1.1; DK 1.2; DP 1.2; DK 1.3; DP 1.3; DK 2.1; DP2.1; DK 2.2; DP 2.2; EK 1.1; EP 1.1 FK 1.1; FP 1.1; FK 1.2; FP 1.2; FK 4.2; FP 4.2
Planning and enabling learning, level four:	
Values and commitments included in the unit:	AS 1; AS 3; AS 4; BS 1; BS 2; BS 3; BS 4; BS 5; CS 1; CS 2; CS 3; DS 1; DS 2; ES 1; FS 1; FS 4
Standards included in the unit:	AK 1.1; AP 1.1; AK 3.1; AP 3.1; AK 4.2; AP 4.2; BK 1.1; BP 1.1; BK 1.2; BP 1.2; BK 2.1; BP 2.1; BK 2.2; BP 2.2; BK 2.3; BP 2.3; BK 2.4; BP 2.4; BK 2.5; BP 2.5; BK 2.6; BP 2.6; BK 3.1; BP 3.1; BK 3.2; BP 3.2; BK 3.3; BP 3.3; BK 3.4; BP 3.4; BK 3.5; BP 3.5; BK 4.1; BP 4.1; BK 5.1; BP 5.1; BK 5.2; BP 5.2; CK 1.1; CP 1.1; CK 2.1; CP 2.1; CK 3.1; CP 3.1; CK 3.2; CP 3.2; CK 3.3; CP 3.3; CK 3.4; CP 3.4; CK3.5; CP 3.5; DK 1.1; DP 1.1; DK 1.2; DP 1.2; DK 1.3; DP 1.3; DK 2.1; DK 2.2; DP 2.1; DP 2.2; EK 1.1; EP 1.1 FK 1.1; FP 1.1; FK 1.2; FP 1.2; FK 4.2; FP 4.2

The New overarching professional standards for teachers, tutors and trainers in the lifelong learning sector
LLUK (2007)
Printed with permission from Lifelong Learning UK
The full standards can be accessed at: http://www.lluk.org.uk/documents/professional_standards_for_itts
_ 020107.pdf

LANGUAGE AND LITERACY

Personal, social and cultural factors influencing language and literacy learning and development:

L1 The different factors affecting the acquisition and development of language and literacy skills
L2 The importance of English language and literacy in enabling users to participate in public life, society and the modern economy
L3 Potential barriers that can hinder development of language skills
L4 The main learning disabilities and difficulties relating to language learning and skill development
L5 Multilingualism and the role of the first language in the acquisition of additional languages
L6 Issues that arise when learning another language or translating from one language to another
L7 Issues related to varieties of English, including standard English, dialects and attitudes towards them
L8 The importance of context in language use and the influence of the communicative situation

Explicit knowledge about language and of the four skills of speaking, listening, reading and writing:

Speaking

LS1 Making appropriate choices in oral communication episodes
LS2 Having a knowledge of fluency, accuracy and competence for ESOL learners
LS3 Using spoken English effectively

Listening

LL1 Listening effectively

Reading

LR1 Interpreting written texts
LR2 Knowledge of how textual features support reading
LR3 Understanding the barriers to accessing text

Writing

LW1   Communicating the writing process
LW2   Using genre to develop writing
LW3   Developing spelling and punctuation skills

Personal language skills:

Speaking

PLS1   Expressing yourself clearly, using communication techniques to help convey meaning and to enhance the delivery and accessibility of the message
PLS2   Showing the ability to use language, style and tone in ways that suit the intended audience, and to recognise their use by others
PLS3   Using appropriate techniques to reinforce oral communication, check how well the information is received and support the understanding of those listening
PLS4   Using non-verbal communication to assist in conveying meaning and receiving information, and recognising its use by others

Listening

PLL1   Listening attentively and responding sensitively to contributions made by others

Reading

PLR1   Find, and select from, a range of reference material and sources of information, including the internet
PLR2   Use and reflect on a range of reading strategies to interpret texts and to locate information or meaning
PLR3   Identify and record the key information or messages contained within reading material using note-taking techniques

Writing

PLW1 Write fluently, accurately and legibly on a range of topics
PLW2 Select appropriate format and style of writing for different purposes and different readers
PLW3 Use spelling and punctuation accurately in order to make meaning clear
PLW4 Understand and use the conventions of grammar (the forms and structures of words, phrases, clauses, sentences and texts) consistently when producing written text

NUMERACY

Personal, social and cultural factors influencing numeracy learning and development:

N1   The different factors affecting the acquisition and development of numeracy skills

N2 The importance of numeracy in enabling users to participate in, and gain access to, society and the modern economy

N3 Potential barriers that hinder development of numeracy skills

N4 The main learning difficulties and disabilities relating to numeracy skills learning and development

N5 The common misconceptions and confusions related to number-associated difficulties

Explicit knowledge of numeracy communication and processes:

Communication

NC1 Making and using decisions about understanding

NC2 Communicating processes, and understandings

Processes

NP1 A knowledge of the capacity of numeracy skills to support problem solving

NP2 Making sense of situations and representing them

NP3 Processing and analysis

NP4 Using numeracy skills and content knowledge

NP5 Interpreting and evaluating results

NP6 Communicating and reflecting on findings

Personal numeracy skills:

Communication

PNC1 Communicate with others about numeracy in an open and supportive manner

PNC2 Assess own, and other people's, understanding

PNC3 Express yourself clearly and accurately

PNC4 Communicate about numeracy in a variety of ways that suit and support the intended audience, and recognise such use by others

PNC5 Use appropriate techniques to reinforce oral communication, check how well the information is received and support understanding of those listening

Processes

PNP1 Use strategies to make sense of a situation requiring the application of numeracy

PNP2 Process and analyse data

PNP3 Use generic content knowledge and skills

PNP4 Make decisions concerning content knowledge and skills

PNP5 Understand the validity of different methods

PNP6 Consider accuracy, efficiency and effectiveness when solving problems and reflect on what has been learned

PNP7 Make sense of data

PNP8 Select appropriate format and style for communicating findings

INFORMATION AND COMMUNICATION TECHNOLOGY (ICT)

Personal, social and cultural factors influencing ICT learning and development:

ICT1   The different factors affecting the acquisition and development of ICT skills

ICT2   The importance of ICT in enabling users to participate in and gain access to society and the modern economy

ICT3   Understanding of the range of learners' technological and educational backgrounds

ICT4   The main learning disabilities and difficulties relating to ICT learning and skill development

ICT5   Potential barriers that inhibit ICT skills development

Explicit knowledge about ICT:

Communication

ICTC1   Making and using decisions about understanding

ICTC2   Communicating processes and understandings

Processes

ICTP1   Purposeful use of ICT

ICTP2   Essential characteristics of ICT

ICTP3   How learners develop ICT skills

Personal ICT skills:

Communication

ICTPC1   Communicate with others with/about ICT in an open and supportive manner

ICTPC2   Assess own, and other people's, understanding

ICTPC3   Express yourself clearly and accurately

ICTPC4   Communicate about/with ICT in a variety of ways that suit and support the intended audience, and recognise such use by others

ICTPC5   Use appropriate techniques to reinforce oral communication, check how well the information is received and support understanding of those listening

Processes

ICTPP1   Using ICT systems

ICTPP2   Finding, selecting and exchanging information

ICTPP3   Developing and presenting information

Addressing literacy, language, numeracy and ICT needs in education and training: Defining
the minimum core of teachers' knowledge, understanding and personal skills – A guide for
initial teacher education programmes
© Crown copyright 2007

Printed with permission from Lifelong Learning UK.

References; for example, ICTPP1, have been added by the authors for ease of
cross-referencing within the chapters.

The full document is available at: http://www.lluk.org.uk/documents/minimum_
core_may_2007_3rd.pdf

A companion guide: *Inclusive learning approaches for literacy, language, numeracy and*
ICT (2007) is available at: http://www.lluk.org.uk/documents/mcg_web.pdf

APPENDIX 3 TIPS FOR TEACHING

- Prepare your session plan in advance, ensuring you use SMART objectives.

- Mentally rehearse your sessions to check your timings.

- Prepare icebreakers/energisers for use as and when required.

- Prepare an extra activity in case you have spare time, or know what you can leave out if you run short of time.

- Check overhead transparencies/presentation slides and handouts for spelling, grammar, punctuation and syntax.

- Plan ahead – practise any planned activities using relevant technology, equipment or resources beforehand, photocopy handouts as required, book equipment if necessary.

- Be prepared, be organised and be professional.

- Have a contingency plan in case something goes wrong or isn't available; for example, handouts as an alternative to your presentation, just in case the equipment doesn't work.

- Have spare pens, paper etc and a watch or clock.

- Arrive early to check the room, equipment and resources.

- Set up the area to suit your topic, so that all learners can see and hear you.

- Inform your learners where facilities such as toilets, refreshments etc are located and make sure they are aware of fire and safety procedures.

- Smile, introduce yourself, your topic and your aim. It is useful to have your aim on the board or on a flipchart/screen which can remain visible throughout your session.

- Use a starter activity if you know some learners may be delayed.

- State your objectives clearly.

- Deliver your topic confidently, remaining focused, in control and professional.

- Project energy, enthusiasm and passion for the subject.

- Pace the session according to your learners, involve them so that the session is centred around them and not you, differentiate learning activities, and take into account any learner difficulties or disabilities.

- Ask open questions (ones that begin with *who, what, when, where, why* and *how*).

- Use your learners' names when speaking to them or asking questions.

- Use eye contact, and stand tall or move around the room and/or sit down to change your eyeline.

- Speak a little more slowly and loudly than usual.

- If you set a group activity, think about what you will be doing while your learners are active, and give them a target completion time.

- Have some extension tasks available for learners who may complete other activities early.

- At the end of your session, allow time for questions from your learners.

- When summarising, recap your aim and ensure that you have covered all your objectives.

- State what will be covered in the next session (if applicable).

- If you are setting any homework, ensure that you give a target date.

- Evaluate yourself afterwards, reflecting what was good, what you could do differently or change for next time.

- Keep your professional development record up to date, arranging any relevant training for yourself.

APPENDIX 4 TEACHING AND LEARNING RESOURCES

Information and learning technologies	Objects
• Audio machine and tapes • Calculators • Camcorder • CD-ROMs • Computers/laptops • Digital cameras • DVDs • Epidiascope • Graphic tablets • Interactive whiteboards • Internet • Intranet • Microscope • Mobile telephone • Personal digital assistants • Photocopier • Projectors • Radio • Recording devices • Scanners • Television • Video conferencing • Video recorder • Virtual learning environment • Voting technology • Webcam • Whiteboards	• Animals • Games • Models • Plants • Puppets • Puzzles • Samples • Specimens • Sports equipment • The *real thing* • Tools • Toys

	People
	• Colleagues: teachers, course leaders, mentors, technicians, clerical and support staff • Friends and relatives • Head of service/centre/organisation, senior management staff • Information/resource centre staff • Learners • Manufacturers/suppliers • Other professionals: internal/external agency staff, verifiers, moderators, exam board/awarding body personnel, vocational experts, visiting speakers • Volunteers • Yourself

Outside events and visits	Visual aids
• Cinema/theatre/concert/art gallery • Conferences • Exhibitions • Field trips • Lectures • Libraries • Museums • Specialist shops • Sports/leisure centres	• Charts/posters • Display board • Flannel/sticky/magnetic boards • Flipchart • Maps • Overhead projector and transparencies • Presentations • Photographs • Whiteboard/chalk board

Resource materials	
• Advertisements • Books • Catalogues • Comics • Handouts • Information notes • Journals • Magazines • Maps	• Manuals • Newspapers • Original documents • Photocopies • Promotional literature • Publicity materials • Quiz • Reports • Wordsquares/crosswords • Worksheets/books